Jesus,
CALM
MY
HEART

Books by Ruth Schwenk
from Bethany House Publishers

Trusting God in All the Things*

Jesus, Calm My Heart

* with Karen Ehman

Jesus, CALM MY HEART

365 PRAYERS TO GIVE YOU PEACE AT THE CLOSE OF EVERY DAY

RUTH SCHWENK

BETHANYHOUSE

a division of Baker Publishing Group
Minneapolis, Minnesota

Published by Bethany House Publishers
Minneapolis, Minnesota
www.bethanyhouse.com

Bethany House Publishers is a division of
Baker Publishing Group, Grand Rapids, Michigan

Printed in China

Library of Congress Cataloging-in-Publication Data
Names: Schwenk, Ruth, author.
Title: Jesus, calm my heart : 365 prayers to give you peace at the close of every day / Ruth Schwenk.
Description: Minneapolis, Minnesota : Bethany House Publishers, a division of Baker Publishing Group, [2023]
Identifiers: LCCN 2023002264 | ISBN 9780764241499 (cloth) | ISBN 9781493443826 (ebook)
Subjects: LCSH: Christian women—Prayers and devotions. | Devotional calendars.
Classification: LCC BV4527 .S279 2023 | DDC 248.8/43—dc23/eng/20230328
LC record available at https://lccn.loc.gov/2023002264

Cover design by Micaela Blankenship

The author is represented by the Brock, Inc. Agency.

Baker Publishing Group publications use paper produced from sustainable forestry practices and post-consumer waste whenever possible.

23   24   25   26   27   28   29   7   6   5   4   3   2   1

CONTENTS

Contents

Contents

Contents

Contents

Contents

Contents

Contents

Contents

Contents

INTRODUCTION

Hi, friend,

A few years ago, I lay in bed thinking of you, my dear reader, and my community online. My mind started racing with all the things I knew you must be facing. So I typed out a simple prayer at around midnight on my Facebook page and hit post. It simply said,

Lord, I pray for the woman reading this right now. Give her wisdom as she seeks to follow You with her whole heart. Help her to not grow weary in the journey but cling to You for her hope and strength. When the world wants more of her, give her peace that You are enough. Cover her with Your grace and be ever near to her, Lord. Amen.

I had no idea what God would do with that simple prayer prayed over you. Thousands of shares and comments poured in as women simply typed back "Amen," or "You have no idea how much I needed that right now." Or, "How did you know exactly what I was thinking?!"

It's true. The daily troubles of life have a way of bringing us to our knees. At night, when we are weary from a long day, words can be difficult to find. We struggle to wrap language around our longings, but what we know is that we need God. The psalmist describes in Psalm 6:6–7 what we've probably all experienced— how the coming to an end of a day can also be the coming to an end of ourselves. We might feel worn out. We groan. Tired and worried, we can weep. And yet this is also where we meet God, who never sleeps, and is waiting to give us His hope, assurance, and joy.

Jesus, Calm My Heart is my invitation for you to experience the peace and friendship God offers as you encounter the One who can do all things. For each of the 365 nights, I've included a prayer written as one that I've prayed over you. In addition, there is also a prayer for you to write in response with your unique situation in mind. Not every prayer will always apply to your situation, but you may know someone you can pass that prayer along to. No matter what, I am confident that as you come to the end of each day, you will encounter the God who loves you and is there for you. You will find Him faithful to meet you each night and give you exactly what you need.

So I invite you to discover all that God has for you as you come to Him. I'm grateful to journey together.

Many blessings,

Ruth

Lord, I pray for the woman reading this right now who **feels stuck in a season of waiting**. Give her patience as she waits and remind her that some of Your greatest work is done amid uncertainty (Isaiah 64:4). You have a plan, and Your plan is good. She can trust You. Help her to use this time to draw closer to You. Fill her with Your peace, cover her with Your grace, and be so near to her tonight, Lord. Amen.

Lord, help me to be patient in the wait and to trust You with . . .

_____

_____

_____

_____

_____

Since ancient times no one has heard, no ear has perceived, no eye has seen any God besides you, who acts on behalf of those who wait for him.

Isaiah 64:4

Lord, I pray for the woman reading this right now who senses she is **spiritually dry**. Would You flood her heart with a sense of Your presence tonight? She wants to want to follow You, but she is struggling. Help her see glimpses of You in her ordinary every day (John 5:17). Renew and reignite her love for You and for Your Word. Give her Your favor and Your peace as she seeks You, Lord. Amen.

Lord, renew my love for You by . . .

_____

_____

_____

_____

_____

In his defense Jesus said to them, "My Father is always at his work to this very day, and I too am working."

John 5:17

Lord, I pray for the woman reading this right now who **feels completely overwhelmed by her life.** Give her peace in the middle of her chaos, Lord. Help her to just take that one next step without looking too far ahead. When she's tempted to look to the left or to the right, remind her to look to You. You will give her the strength she needs, and You will sustain her (Isaiah 46:4). She can trust You. Be her Shepherd as she follows closely after You, Lord. Amen.

Lord, bring peace to my . . .

_____

_____

_____

_____

Even to your old age and gray hairs I am he, I am he who will sustain you. I have made you and I will carry you; I will sustain you and I will rescue you.

Isaiah 46:4

night
4

Lord, I pray for the woman reading this right now who **is hoping and praying You will come through for her**. Comfort her in the middle of what seems impossible to her and give her strength to walk with You no matter what (Isaiah 40:29). Fill her with Your peace and settle her with Your assurance. You love her, and You won't let her go. Show her Your faithfulness as she draws near to You, Lord. Amen.

Lord, help me to remain steadfast in the middle of . . .

_____

_____

_____

_____

_____

He gives strength to the weary and increases the power of the weak.

Isaiah 40:29

Lord, I pray for the woman reading this right now who **is struggling to keep her head and her heart in a good place.** Help her to cling to Your Word and Your truths no matter how she feels or what her thoughts tell her. Give her courage to seek help if she needs it, and may she feel absolutely no shame in reaching out for support. You are the God of hope, and she can trust Your plans to prosper her and not to harm her (Jeremiah 29:11). May the days ahead be bright as she leans on You, Lord. Amen.

Lord, give me grace and courage to . . .

_____

_____

_____

_____

"For I know the plans I have for you," declares the Lord, "plans to prosper you and not to harm you, plans to give you hope and a future."

Jeremiah 29:11

Lord, I pray for the woman reading this right now who **is wrestling with regret**. Remind her, Lord, that even though we mess up, You are the God of redemption. Encourage her with the truth of Jesus' love and forgiveness. You hold her world in Your hands, and You have a plan for her. So help her to look forward, not backward. You have redeemed her, and she can walk with courage and confidence in Your loving care (Isaiah 43:1). Freedom is Your gift to her tonight. Reveal Your love to her and cover her with Your grace, Lord. Amen.

Lord, in my struggle with regret, help me to let go of . . .

_____

_____

_____

But now, this is what the Lord says—he who created you, Jacob, he who formed you, Israel: "Do not fear, for I have redeemed you; I have summoned you by name; you are mine."

Isaiah 43:1

Lord, I pray for the woman reading this right now who **is weary**. Help her to turn her burdens over to You completely. You, Lord, are her true and enduring Rest. Give her the strength to not give up or give in. Fortify her with Your love for her. Give her eyes to see past her current struggle. And protect her heart from growing hard or heavy. By Your grace, keep her heart tender and open to all that You have for her. Bring her life and peace as she walks with You, Lord. Amen.

Lord, give me strength to . . .

_____

_____

_____

_____

_____

I will refresh the weary and satisfy the faint.

Jeremiah 31:25

Lord, I pray for the woman reading this right now who **is struggling to find joy in this season.** She knows she *should* have that deep-down joy in You, but she just doesn't feel it. Make her aware of Your presence and comfort her heart tonight. Remind her that You see her, and You love her so very much (Jeremiah 31:3). Fill her with inexpressible joy. Show her glimpses of hope in the midst of her heartache and give her a reason to smile, even tonight, Lord. Amen.

Lord, help me to find joy in . . .

_____

_____

_____

_____

The LORD appeared to us in the past, saying: "I have loved you with an everlasting love; I have drawn you with unfailing kindness."

Jeremiah 31:3

Lord, I pray for the woman reading this right now who **is miserable.** Her life has been so hard for so long, and she's in need of respite. Restore her and deliver her. Be her help in trouble, Lord. Set her feet on solid ground and fill her with the joy she once had. Bless her and keep her close to You. You have good for her in the days ahead, and she can depend on You, Lord. Amen.

Lord, even though life is hard, I am believing You for . . .

_____

_____

_____

_____

The Lord is a refuge for the oppressed, a stronghold in times of trouble. Those who know your name trust in you, for you, Lord, have never forsaken those who seek you.

Psalm 9:9–10

night
10

Lord, I pray for the woman reading this right now who **is experiencing anxiety.** Whatever fears she has, we know You can calm them. We know that nothing takes You by surprise, Lord. You are her Sovereign Father, and nothing is too hard for You (Genesis 18:14). Bring an unexplainable peace over her tonight. Help her to lay her worries at Your feet and trust that You will take care of her. Give her a night of restful sleep and help her wake up feeling encouraged and hopeful, Lord. Amen.

Lord, help me to trust You with . . .

_____

_____

_____

_____

Is anything too hard for the LORD? I will return to you at the appointed time next year, and Sarah will have a son.

Genesis 18:14

Lord, I pray for the woman reading this right now who **needs to know You are with her tonight.** Make Your presence known to her, Lord. And even if she can't feel Your presence, remind her of Your promise to never leave her or forsake her (Hebrews 13:5). You see her right where she is. Comfort her, hold her, and help her. Be a refuge for her and help her not to be shaken. Draw close to her as she clings to You, Lord. Amen.

Lord, give me faith to see You in . . .

_____

_____

_____

_____

Keep your lives free from the love of money and be content with what you have, because God has said, "Never will I leave you; never will I forsake you."

Hebrews 13:5

night
12

Lord, I pray for the woman reading this right now who **feels desperate for Your peace**. Please bring calm in the midst of her chaos, Lord. Even when our circumstances feel out of control, You are in control. Help her to trust You and remember that nothing is an emergency to You (Isaiah 26:3). You have her world in Your hands, and You will take care of her. Settle her heart and give her Your peace tonight, Lord. Amen.

Lord, give me peace with . . .

_____

_____

_____

_____

You will keep in perfect peace those whose minds are steadfast, because they trust in you.

Isaiah 26:3

Lord, I pray for the woman reading this right now who **has a mind spinning with what-ifs**. Remind her that there is nothing she is facing that You don't already have in Your care. Help her to turn her worries over to You in worship—to unspin her spinning mind. Remind her of Your wisdom, that it is unending and beyond measure (Romans 11:33). Be so very close to her as she brings her worries to You, Lord. Amen.

Lord, free my spinning mind from . . .

_____

_____

_____

_____

_____

Oh, the depth of the riches of the wisdom and knowledge of God! How unsearchable his judgments, and his paths beyond tracing out!

Romans 11:33

night
14

Lord, I pray for the woman reading this right now who **is struggling with change**. Remind her tonight, Lord, that there is nothing in her life that You aren't working through. Even though she is in the midst of change, You are an unchangeable God (Hebrews 13:8). Although she may not see it now, You have a good plan for her, and she can trust You. Give her peace and help her to have confidence that You will come through for her, Lord. Amen.

Lord, give me the grace to release . . .

_____

_____

_____

_____

_____

Jesus Christ is the same yesterday and today and forever.

Hebrews 13:8

Lord, I pray for the woman reading this right now who **remains in a season of waiting.** Give her patience as she waits and remind her that some of Your greatest work is done in seasons of uncertainty. Teach her not to rush this season or set of circumstances. Reveal to her the way You are working in her heart during this time (Isaiah 40:31). Help her to lean in and move closer to You, Lord. Amen.

Lord, teach me to wait well by . . .

_____

_____

_____

_____

But those who hope in the LORD will renew their strength. They will soar on wings like eagles; they will run and not grow weary, they will walk and not be faint.

Isaiah 40:31

night
16

Lord, I pray for the woman reading this right now who **just needs a break**. Give her relief in the midst of her distress. Breathe new life into her. Breathe *Your* life into her. You desire for her to have life to the fullest (John 10:10). She can rest in Your care and find solace in You. Help her to walk calmly and confidently as she trusts You with each and every day, Lord. Amen.

Lord, give me relief from . . .

_____

_____

_____

_____

_____

The thief comes only to steal and kill and destroy; I have come that they may have life, and have it to the full.

John 10:10

Lord, I pray for the woman reading this right now who **is struggling with worry**. Fill her with Your perfect peace that surpasses all understanding (Philippians 4:7). Remind her that nothing is impossible for You. Whatever circumstances she is facing, she can trust You. You go before her and behind her and on every side. Her life is safe with You. Be near to her and comfort her tonight, Lord. Amen.

Lord, fill me with the confidence that You are . . .

_____

_____

_____

_____

Do not be anxious about anything, but in every situation, by prayer and petition, with thanksgiving, present your requests to God. And the peace of God, which transcends all understanding, will guard your hearts and your minds in Christ Jesus.

Philippians 4:6–7

night
18

Lord, I pray for the woman reading this right now who **is questioning the call You have on her life.** Give her the courage to take that step of faith You are calling her to take no matter how she feels. She can walk boldly when she keeps in step with You because You will be her strength. Help her to trust You will be beside her every step of the way (Joshua 1:9). Be her peace and remind her that she is not alone, Lord. Amen.

Lord, give me the courage to . . .

_____

_____

_____

_____

Have I not commanded you? Be strong and courageous. Do not be afraid; do not be discouraged, for the LORD your God will be with you wherever you go.

Joshua 1:9

Lord, I pray for the woman reading this right now who **feels lost.**
Remind her that You are her anchor, Lord. She is not alone. Nor
is she walking aimlessly. Help her to tether her life to You. You are
steady and true. Whoever follows You does not walk in darkness,
but in the Light (John 8:12). Give her direction and show her Your
perfect way, Lord. Amen.

Lord, in my aimlessness, I surrender . . .

_____

_____

_____

_____

*When Jesus spoke again to the people, he said, "I am the light of the
world. Whoever follows me will never walk in darkness, but will have
the light of life."*

John 8:12

night
20

Lord, I pray for the woman reading this right now who **feels discouraged**. Remind her that no disappointment is too big for You. You see her, You know her, and You love her. You hold every detail of her life in Your hands, and You have good things for her. Give her comfort and peace as she surrenders outcomes to You and learns to trust in Your plan instead of her own (Proverbs 3:5–6). Help her to lean wholly on You tonight, Lord. Amen.

Lord, help me overcome my discouragement by . . .

_____

_____

_____

_____

Trust in the LORD with all your heart and lean not on your own understanding; in all your ways submit to him, and he will make your paths straight.

Proverbs 3:5–6

Lord, I pray for the woman reading this who **feels unsettled by her circumstances**. Help her to look to You for her security and not the things that threaten to steal her peace. Give her courage as she faces unknowns. Surround her, protect her, and provide for her. Be her strength, Lord (Psalm 28:7). She needs You. May she experience an unexplainable calm tonight as she sleeps, Lord. Amen.

Lord, my heart is unsettled, and I need You to . . .

_____

_____

_____

_____

_____

The LORD is my strength and my shield; my heart trusts in him, and he helps me. My heart leaps for joy, and with my song I praise him.

Psalm 28:7

night
22

Lord, I pray for the woman reading this right now who **is questioning Your goodness**. Life can rattle us sometimes, Lord, and she needs to see You come through for her (Psalm 27:13). Be her provision and give her hope. Encourage her with good news. Give her Your peace and remind her of Your unfailing love, Lord. Amen.

Lord, show me Your goodness by . . .

_____

_____

_____

_____

_____

I remain confident of this: I will see the goodness of the Lord in the land of the living.

Psalm 27:13

Lord, I pray for the woman reading this right now who **feels things will never change**. Give her grace to persevere. To keep going. Help her not to focus only on the current struggle but to see through it. Give her eyes to see the fruit that can come—and will come—if she doesn't give up. Remind her that You are the God who provides everything she needs (Philippians 4:19). May she trust Your unwavering faithfulness to her, Lord. Amen.

Lord, I need Your power to persevere in . . .

_____

_____

_____

_____

And my God will meet all your needs according to the riches of his glory in Christ Jesus.

Philippians 4:19

night
24

Lord, I pray for the woman reading this right now who **fears an unknown future**. Give her strength to lay all that worries her at Your feet (1 Peter 5:7). Remind her that she can trust You with the days ahead. You love her and want the best for her. Pour out Your hope as You pour out Your Spirit in and upon her. Be so close to her and comfort her tonight, Lord. Amen.

Lord, I surrender the unknown of . . .

_____

_____

_____

_____

_____

Cast all your anxiety on him because he cares for you.

1 Peter 5:7

Lord, I pray for the woman reading this right now who **feels invisible**. Give her assurance that You see her right where she is (Genesis 16:13). Don't let the enemy steal the gift she is with discouragement. Give her assurance to live as You see her—a deeply cherished and beautiful child of God. You love her so much, and she can rest in that truth tonight, Lord. Amen.

Lord, help me to live for Your approval by . . .

She gave this name to the LORD who spoke to her: "You are the God who sees me," for she said, "I have now seen the One who sees me."

Genesis 16:13

night
26

Lord, I pray for the woman reading this right now who **is facing unimaginable circumstances**. Give her assurance of Your faithfulness and confidence that this season will not last forever. Remind her that absolutely nothing takes You by surprise, and that You are right there with her. You won't let her go. Comfort her and cover her with Your loving care tonight, Lord. Amen.

Lord, help me to find comfort in You as I face . . .

_____

_____

_____

_____

_____

Even there your hand will guide me, your right hand will hold me fast.

Psalm 139:10

Lord, I pray for the woman reading this right now who **is struggling to discern what is next.** As she waits and seeks what You want, teach her to be faithful right where she is. When she is tempted to run ahead of You, remind her that You have a perfect plan and that You are working right where You have her as she waits. Give her wisdom and open her eyes to see what You have for her. Help her to keep in step with You, and surround her with Your peace, Lord. Amen.

Lord, as I wait, teach me to . . .

_____

_____

_____

_____

_____

*Be still before the L*ORD *and wait patiently for him.*

Psalm 37:7

night
28

Lord, I pray for the woman reading this right now who **desperately wants to change but wonders if she ever will**. Give her eyes to see how far she has come. Who she is today is not who she was. Remind her that change is possible with You. You love her unconditionally, and she has a future with You. Help her to keep her eyes on Jesus, the Author and Perfecter of her faith. He is making her new, in His time and in His way. Cover her with Your grace as she seeks to be obedient to You, Lord. Amen.

Lord, I will keep my eyes on Jesus by . . .

_____

_____

_____

_____

See, the former things have taken place, and new things I declare; before they spring into being I announce them to you.

Isaiah 42:9

night
29

Lord, I pray for the woman reading this right now who **feels the hard times will never end**. Give her comfort tonight, Lord. Remind her that no matter what she faces or how long she faces it, she can trust You. You see her. You love her. And You will not leave her. Help her to see glimpses of hope and Your goodness in the midst of her suffering. Be so close to her and comfort her tonight, Lord. Amen.

Lord, guard my heart from growing weary in . . .

_____

_____

_____

_____

_____

My comfort in my suffering is this: Your promise preserves my life.

Psalm 119:50

night
30

Lord, I pray for the woman reading this right now **who finally feels hopeful and at peace.** She was always weary and wondering if life would get better. But she has chosen now to find her strength in You even when life isn't perfect. Everything won't always be all right, and that is okay. You love her so much, and lasting joy is found in her relationship with You. Help her to keep being faithful and surrender outcomes to You. Give her wisdom and courage to trust You each day, Lord. Amen.

Lord, I need You to remind me of . . .

_____

_____

_____

_____

Then I will go to the altar of God, to God, my joy and my delight.

Psalm 43:4

Lord, I pray for the woman reading this right now who **is desperate for Your peace in her life.** No matter the chaos around her, settle her soul and calm her heart tonight. Overwhelm her with Your presence and give her hope. You are the Lord of peace, who gives peace at all times and in every way (2 Thessalonians 3:16). She has no reason to fear. Remind her that You love her and You are right beside her, Lord. Amen.

Lord, regardless of the chaos around me, help me to understand . . .

_____

_____

_____

_____

Now may the Lord of peace himself give you peace at all times and in every way. The Lord be with all of you.

2 Thessalonians 3:16

night
32

Lord, I pray for the woman reading this right now who **is living a life that looks nothing like she thought it would.** Help her to see that what You have for her is better. Remind her that You bring beauty out of the hard stuff, Lord. Help her to hold on to hope and to trust You. You have a plan for her, and Your plan is good (Isaiah 46:10–11). Give her courage to live each day fully and in peace as she rests in Your purposes for her, Lord. Amen.

Lord, fill me with Your Spirit to fully embrace . . .

I make known the end from the beginning, from ancient times, what is still to come. . . . What I have said, that I will bring about; what I have planned, that I will do.

Isaiah 46:10–11

Lord, I pray for the woman reading this right now who **is gripped by fear**. Remind her tonight, Lord, that You see her and won't leave her. Whatever it is that worries her is no match for Your goodness and Your power. You can deliver her from *all* fears (Psalm 34:4–5). Give her comfort in knowing that, even as she sleeps, You are fighting for her. She can trust that You are with her tonight, Lord. Amen.

Lord, I will not fear tomorrow because I know . . .

_____

_____

_____

_____

_____

I sought the Lord, and he answered me; he delivered me from all my fears. Those who look to him are radiant; their faces are never covered with shame.

Psalm 34:4–5

night
34

Lord, I pray for the woman reading this right now who **is feeling discouraged by her current circumstances.** She feels like things will never change, and she is tired of the same old thing, Lord. Give her courage to sit in this hard and uncomfortable season with eyes open to what You have for her. Soften her heart toward You and what You desire for her (Psalm 32:8). Comfort her, be her peace, and bring her hope for better days to come, Lord. Amen.

Lord, give me the strength to overcome my discouragement with . . .

_____

_____

_____

_____

I will instruct you and teach you in the way you should go; I will counsel you with my loving eye on you.

Psalm 32:8

Lord, I pray for the woman who **is struggling to place her plans in Your hands.** Help her to surrender to You tonight, Lord. Empower her to release her plans for Your purposes. You love her, and You want what is best for her. She can absolutely trust You to do far more with her life than she can imagine (Ephesians 3:20). Cover her with Your peace as she follows Your will and way, Lord. Amen.

Lord, empower me to surrender my . . .

_____

_____

_____

_____

_____

Now to him who is able to do immeasurably more than all we ask or imagine, according to his power that is at work within us.

Ephesians 3:20

night
36

Lord, I pray for the woman reading this right now who **is barely hanging on**. She needs you right now, Lord. Remind her that her current reality is not her final reality. Enable her to persevere even when she feels like giving up. Sustain her in her darkness and give her the grace to take another step. You are beside her and she can find her strength in You. Help her to feel Your presence so very near tonight, Lord. Amen.

Lord, please give me the grace in my struggle to . . .

_____

_____

_____

_____

_____

Consider him who endured such opposition from sinners, so that you will not grow weary and lose heart.

Hebrews 12:3

Lord, I pray for the woman reading this right now who **is doubting You can actually use her.** Remind her right now, Lord, that she is Your daughter. You have given her gifts, and the gifts You have given her are good (1 Peter 4:10). Protect her from the fear and uncertainty that can so easily creep in. Give her the courage to step out in faith into what You have for her. And help her to lean on You as she follows Your plan, Lord. Amen.

Lord, give me the courage to step out in faith by . . .

_____

_____

_____

_____

Each of you should use whatever gift you have received to serve others, as faithful stewards of God's grace in its various forms.

1 Peter 4:10

night
38

Lord, I pray for the woman reading this right now who **wonders if You are even listening.** Give her assurance that You hear her prayers. Remind her that You see her, You know her, and You love her beyond comprehension (Psalm 139:1–3). Every detail of her life matters to You. Even when she can't see it, You are working in her life, and You will take care of her. Be so near to her tonight as she trusts in You, Lord. Amen.

Lord, I'm struggling to hear You. Help me to trust that . . .

_____

_____

_____

_____

You have searched me, Lord, and you know me. You know when I sit and when I rise; you perceive my thoughts from afar. You discern my going out and my lying down; you are familiar with all my ways.

Psalm 139:1–3

Lord, I pray for the woman reading this right now who **isn't sure how she can face the mountain ahead** of her. Help her to take the next step. Just one step at a time (Psalm 37:23–24). Give her courage and boldness that can only come from You. Fill her with unwavering faith and give her grace to honor You even when it is hard. May she walk faithfully in this trying season, Lord. Amen.

Lord, I need Your help to climb . . .

_____

_____

_____

_____

_____

The LORD makes firm the steps of the one who delights in him; though he may stumble, he will not fall, for the LORD upholds him with his hand.

Psalm 37:23–24

night
40

Lord, I pray for the woman reading this right now who **is battling depression**. Deliver her from sadness and fill her instead with joy. Give her the courage and wisdom to reach out for help. Enable her to see there is no shame in leaning on others and seeking care (Ecclesiastes 4:9–10). She is wise and brave to do so! Help her to experience glimpses of Your hope and joy tonight, Lord. Amen.

Lord, help me in my depression to lean on others and seek help by . . .

_____

_____

_____

_____

_____

Two are better than one, because they have a good return for their labor:
If either of them falls down, one can help the other up.

Ecclesiastes 4:9–10

Lord, I pray for the woman reading this right now who **is struggling to understand Your plan for her life.** Remind her that she is of immense value and worth to You. Reveal to her the areas You have gifted her in and make plain her path forward. You are sovereign over her days, and she can trust You to lead her. Help her to rest and know that You are with her, Lord. Amen.

Lord, give me clarity and direction in . . .

_____

_____

_____

_____

_____

And even the very hairs of your head are all numbered. So don't be afraid; you are worth more than many sparrows.

Matthew 10:30–31

night
42

Lord, I pray for the woman reading this right now who **feels lonely**. Turn her eyes to You and all she has in You, Lord. You know what it is like to be left alone, forgotten, and misunderstood (Mark 10:33–34). Give her comfort and peace. Remind her that You see her at this moment, right where she is. You are a friend to her, and she can lean wholly on You. Overwhelm her with Your care and Your favor, Lord. Amen.

Lord, when I feel alone, I will . . .

_____

_____

_____

_____

The Son of Man will be delivered over to the chief priests and the teachers of the law. They will condemn him to death and will hand him over to the Gentiles, who will mock him and spit on him, flog him and kill him.

Mark 10:33–34

Lord, I pray for the woman reading this right now who **is fearful of what is to come.** She needs Your peace right now, Lord. Remind her that she can rest in Your care tonight because You will take care of her tomorrow. Give her courage, strength, and hope as she trusts in You. Comfort her in her time of need and cover her with Your loving hand tonight, Lord. Amen.

Lord, I'm struggling with what is ahead. Help me not to be afraid of . . .

_____

_____

_____

_____

_____

Therefore do not worry about tomorrow, for tomorrow will worry about itself. Each day has enough trouble of its own.

Matthew 6:34

night
44

Lord, I pray for the woman reading this right now who **wonders if her pain has any purpose**. Guard her heart against the enemy's lies. Help her to understand that there is always meaning and purpose in what we are walking through, even if we never see it. Give her wisdom to see that if there was fruit in Jesus' suffering, there is fruit in her suffering (1 Peter 5:10). You have a purpose and a plan, and she can trust You. Be so near to her tonight as she places her hope in You, Lord. Amen.

Lord, I will resist the enemy in my pain by . . .

_____

_____

_____

_____

And the God of all grace, who called you to his eternal glory in Christ, after you have suffered a little while, will himself restore you and make you strong, firm and steadfast.

1 Peter 5:10

Lord, I pray for the woman reading this right now who **is wrestling with how she can make a difference.** Help her not to dwell on "what could be" but embrace "what is" now. You have given her good gifts, and You can use her for Your glory. Remind her that her work is for You and not for men as she serves You (Colossians 3:23–24). Give her eyes to see the opportunities all around her, Lord. Amen.

Lord, teach me to do the everyday things with . . .

_____

_____

_____

_____

Whatever you do, work at it with all your heart, as working for the Lord, not for human masters, since you know that you will receive an inheritance from the Lord as a reward. It is the Lord Christ you are serving.

Colossians 3:23–24

night
46

Lord, I pray for the woman reading this right now who **is struggling with thoughts that are running wild.** Help her to release everything she can't control. Holy Spirit, fill her with peace and take hold of her thoughts (Philippians 4:7). Don't let her mind wander or panic. But instead, let her mind be tamed by Your loving care, power, and wisdom. Cover her with Your grace as she seeks Your peace, Lord. Amen.

Lord, when my thoughts run wild, I will . . .

And the peace of God, which transcends all understanding, will guard your hearts and your minds in Christ Jesus.

Philippians 4:7

Lord, I pray for the woman reading this right now who **is laboring to see through the fog.** She wants to follow You, but she feels unsettled and unsure as she seeks Your will. She needs Your peace, Lord. May Your Word be a lamp to her feet and a light for her path (Psalm 119:105). Give her eyes to see this time as an opportunity to grow closer to You and learn from You. Help her not to run ahead of You but to keep in step with what You have for her. Be so near to her tonight, Lord. Amen.

Lord, even though the way seems murky and dim, I will . . .

_____

_____

_____

_____

Your word is a lamp for my feet, a light on my path.

Psalm 119:105

night
48

Lord, I pray for the woman who **is wrestling with the "whys."** Why did this happen? Why is this going on? Help her to let go, surrender, and even forgive. Instead of asking why, help her to begin asking "now what?" Give her the grace to begin anew, honoring You and pleasing You no matter what. Be her joy and her strength as she follows You (Romans 15:13). Overwhelm her with Your love as she trusts in You, Lord. Amen.

Lord, I need your grace to let go of . . .

_____

_____

_____

_____

May the God of hope fill you with all joy and peace as you trust in him, so that you may overflow with hope by the power of the Holy Spirit.

Romans 15:13

night
49

Lord, I pray for the woman reading this right now who **feels she can't go on**. She is weary and worn, and she needs Your strength, Lord. Help her to have faith for what feels impossible. You see her, and You love her. Overwhelm her with Your comfort and Your care. Give her eyes to see Your goodness amid heartache. Fill her heart with hope for tomorrow as she trusts You tonight, Lord. Amen.

Lord, I am not strong enough to carry . . .

_____

_____

_____

_____

_____

There is surely a future hope for you, and your hope will not be cut off.

Proverbs 23:18

night
50

Lord, I pray for the woman reading this right now who **has a deep desire to serve You but doesn't know where to begin.** She needs Your leading and direction, Lord. Speak to her and show her the next step she needs to take. Open doors for her and help her walk with courage as she follows You. You have called her and gifted her. Show her how she can best love You and love others well, Lord. Amen.

Lord, I will take the next step of following You by . . .

_____

_____

_____

_____

_____

Then I heard the voice of the Lord saying, "Whom shall I send? And who will go for us?" And I said, "Here am I. Send me!"

Isaiah 6:8

night
51

Lord, I pray for the woman reading this right now who **is struggling with boundaries**. Help her to see that boundaries are meant to keep her together. They are meant to enable her to give others the best of who she is. Free her from unnecessary guilt and the expectations of others. Give her wisdom to set boundaries that will allow her to live from a healthy place with a healthy heart. Give her courage as she seeks to make changes, Lord. Amen.

Lord, show me how to set boundaries with . . .

_____

_____

_____

_____

Look carefully then how you walk, not as unwise but as wise, making the best use of the time, because the days are evil.

Ephesians 5:15–16 ESV

night
52

Lord, I pray for the woman reading this right now who **is in a season of suffering that seems unending.** She is tired and weary from the long road. Give her the strength to endure what she is facing and the wisdom to navigate the unknowns. Help her to surrender to You the heavy load she is carrying and trust You will take care of her. She needs Your comfort, Your hope, and Your peace. Bring her good news and show her Your faithfulness, Lord. Amen.

Lord, help me remember Your faithfulness in my suffering by . . .

_____

_____

_____

_____

Blessed is the one who perseveres under trial because, having stood the test, that person will receive the crown of life that the Lord has promised to those who love him.

James 1:12

Lord, I pray for the woman reading this right now who **is longing for community**. Surround her with the right friends while protecting her from the wrong ones. Give her the courage to reach out and create the community she is longing for. Help her to be a friend first to those around her, loving others because of Your love for her (1 John 4:19). Help her to find her ultimate satisfaction in Your friendship. Even in times of loneliness, she can lean on Your care, Lord. Amen.

Lord, I will take the step of being a friend first by . . .

_____

_____

_____

_____

_____

We love because he first loved us.

1 John 4:19

night
54

Lord, I pray for the woman reading this right now who **feels discouraged because it seems like everyone else is thriving except her.** She feels trapped in an endless cycle of the same day over and over and she wonders if what she is doing even matters. Open her eyes to the ways You are working in her and through her right now. Show her Your provision in her life. Help her to walk confidently and contentedly where You have her. Encourage her heart and help her to trust You, Lord. Amen.

Lord, I will wait on You because . . .

_____

_____

_____

I will lead the blind by ways they have not known, along unfamiliar paths I will guide them; I will turn the darkness into light before them and make the rough places smooth. These are the things I will do; I will not forsake them.

Isaiah 42:16

Lord, I pray for the woman reading this right now who **is struggling to surrender her circumstances to You**. She is walking through a hard season, and she wonders how she will get through the days ahead. You say Your way is better, Lord, but she can't see a good path ahead. Give her strength and help her to lean on You in the unknown. Remind her that You love her and are with her. She can trust You. Cover her with Your grace and show her Your goodness, Lord. Amen.

Lord, I surrender to You . . .

_____

_____

_____

_____

_____

Commit your way to the LORD; trust in him and he will do this.

Psalm 37:5

night
56

Lord, I pray for the woman reading this right now who **is heartbroken**. She can't understand why her life looks like this or how to go on, and she needs You. Bring peace to her weary soul, Lord. Help her to turn to You with everything that she is, and comfort her (Psalm 34:18). Give her enough strength for today and the courage to take another step tomorrow. Overwhelm her with Your presence as she clings to You tonight, Lord. Amen.

Lord, comfort my heart and bring me peace as I face . . .

_____

_____

_____

_____

The LORD is close to the brokenhearted and saves those who are crushed in spirit.

Psalm 34:18

Lord, I pray for the woman reading this right now who **lacks focus and resolve**. She feels she is wandering, and she is struggling to find her way. Give her clarity, Lord. Show her what to focus on and what to let go of. Don't let her be sidetracked by distractions. But instead, give her greater devotion to what You have placed right in front of her. Be faithful to her as she follows You, Lord. Amen.

Lord, help me to say no to the distraction of . . .

_____

_____

_____

_____

_____

Let your eyes look straight ahead; fix your gaze directly before you.

Proverbs 4:25

night
58

Lord, I pray for the woman reading this right now who **is seeking Your wisdom**. You promised that if we ask, You will give us the wisdom we need (James 1:5). And so, Lord, direct her steps and go before her. Help her to turn her heart toward Your truth alone. Guard her against error and fill her with knowledge beyond her years. Illuminate her path and make it straight as she seeks You, Lord. Amen.

Lord, I need Your wisdom to . . .

_____

_____

_____

_____

_____

If any of you lacks wisdom, you should ask God, who gives generously to all without finding fault, and it will be given to you.

James 1:5

Lord, I pray for the woman reading this right now who **feels unwanted**. Pursue her with Your love in this moment, Lord. Satisfy her with Your delight in her and draw near to her as she draws near to You (James 4:8). Speak to her so that she might be filled with Your Spirit. Remind her that You created her, that You delight in her, and that You have promised never to leave her. Be so close to her tonight, Lord. Amen.

Lord, help me to rest in Your love for me no matter how I feel by . . .

_____

_____

_____

_____

_____

Come near to God and he will come near to you.

James 4:8

night
60

Lord, I pray for the woman reading this right now who **feels powerless over her circumstances**. She is struggling to understand all that is happening to her, and she needs to know You are with her. Give her strength and courage to endure the hard stuff she is facing. You are in complete control of every detail of her life. Help her to cling to You first and trust You will take care of her (Psalm 63:8). Be her hope and be her help tonight, Lord. Amen.

Lord, give me the faith to trust You with . . .

_____

_____

_____

_____

_____

I cling to you; your right hand upholds me.

Psalm 63:8

Lord, I pray for the woman reading this right now who **is struggling to see the good in her life.** It seems You are answering everyone else's prayers but hers, and she needs to know You hear her. Give her hope, Lord. Remind her that You are her Father. You see what she cannot yet see. Your love for her is unending, and You want good things for her. Help her to believe that, Lord. Amen.

*Lord, I know You have good things for me,
and I know You love me because . . .*

_____

_____

_____

_____

"For my thoughts are not your thoughts, neither are your ways my ways," declares the LORD. *"As the heavens are higher than the earth, so are my ways higher than your ways and my thoughts than your thoughts."*

Isaiah 55:8–9

night
62

Lord, I pray for the woman reading this right now who **feels unsettled.** She is longing for something different, but she can't seem to figure out what that is. Help her to cling to You first and foremost. You are what she needs most right now. Show her that her deepest satisfaction can only be found in You (John 6:35). Give her Your peace, cover her with Your grace, and be so near to her tonight, Lord. Amen.

Lord, I know I will never be truly settled until You . . .

Then Jesus declared, "I am the bread of life. Whoever comes to me will never go hungry, and whoever believes in me will never be thirsty."

John 6:35

Lord, I pray for the woman reading this right now who **is suffering in the middle of heartbreak**. Give her grace as she mourns what has been lost. In her pain, draw her heart to Yours. Comfort her and give her hope for what is next, what is yet to come (Psalm 147:3). Be an overwhelming blanket of peace upon her as she trusts You for good things. Soften her heart and help her to see how You are using this season in her life as she moves forward, Lord. Amen.

Lord, comfort me in my feelings of . . .

_____

_____

_____

_____

_____

He heals the brokenhearted and binds up their wounds.

Psalm 147:3

night
64

Lord, I pray for the woman reading this right now who **feels nervous about her future**. Show her that with You, she has nothing to fear. You have promised Your presence no matter what the future holds. You are with her today, and You will be with her tomorrow. You will strengthen her, help her, and uphold her with your righteous right hand (Isaiah 41:10). Comfort her and give her faith to keep following You, Lord. Amen.

Lord, even though I can't see it now, I trust You with . . .

_____

_____

_____

_____

So do not fear, for I am with you; do not be dismayed, for I am your God. I will strengthen you and help you; I will uphold you with my righteous right hand.

Isaiah 41:10

Lord, I pray for the woman reading this right now who **just can't seem to get it all together.** She feels all over the place, and she is longing for peace. Remind her that she is doing the best she can, and she can trust You to do the rest. You will give her exactly what she needs to accomplish what You have for her (2 Corinthians 9:8). Teach her to begin again, with Your help, when she fails. Guard her heart against discouragement as she serves You, Lord. Amen.

Lord, help me to depend more on You by . . .

_____

_____

_____

_____

And God is able to bless you abundantly, so that in all things at all times, having all that you need, you will abound in every good work.

2 Corinthians 9:8

night
66

Lord, I pray for the woman reading this right now who **is struggling to find her voice**. She is doubting herself and wondering what she has to offer. Give her the eyes to see how You have uniquely gifted her, Lord. She can speak life and help those in need in a way others cannot. Fill her with Your Spirit as she takes a step of faith to serve You and those around her. Help her to walk with courage and boldness in this ministry You have for her, Lord. Amen.

Lord, I believe You are calling me to . . .

_____

_____

_____

_____

For the Spirit God gave us does not make us timid, but gives us power, love and self-discipline.

2 Timothy 1:7

Lord, I pray for the woman reading this right now who **is laboring to let go**. No matter how hard she tries, she can't seem to surrender her circumstances to You. Help her to see that there is freedom in letting go instead of holding on. Show her that You can be trusted and counted on. You have wisdom, power, and resources well beyond her own. Be so near to her tonight as she surrenders to You, Lord. Amen.

Lord, give me the grace to let go of . . .

_____

_____

_____

_____

_____

Lord, I know that people's lives are not their own; it is not for them to direct their steps.

Jeremiah 10:23

night
68

Lord, I pray for the woman reading this right now who **is struggling to see You in her hurt**. Her heart is heavy, and she needs You. Lift the burden she is carrying, Lord. Restore her joy and remind her of Your deep love for her. She can give her burdens to You, and You will take care of her. You won't let her slip or fall (Psalm 55:22). Soothe her soul with your lovingkindness tonight, Lord. Amen.

Lord, I will not become discouraged because I know . . .

_____

_____

_____

_____

_____

Cast your cares on the LORD and he will sustain you; he will never let the righteous be shaken.

Psalm 55:22

Lord, I pray for the woman reading this right now who **longs for something more.** She feels hungry and thirsty for meaning. Teach her to first hunger and thirst for You. Give her what her heart needs most—more of Your life within her. You have created her for good works prepared in advance, especially for her (Ephesians 2:10). Fill her and help her to find peace in following You, Lord. Amen.

Lord, in my longing, I will not turn to . . .

_____

_____

_____

_____

_____

For we are God's handiwork, created in Christ Jesus to do good works, which God prepared in advance for us to do.

Ephesians 2:10

night
70

Lord, I pray for the woman reading this right now who **feels confused about where You have her**. She thought You were leading her to this place, but now she feels so unsure. Teach her to be patient, to believe that You have her where she is for a reason. And that even now You are at work changing her and preparing her for what is to come. Help her to find security in knowing that You are faithful and that she can trust You, Lord. Amen.

Lord, I trust that You are at work even in . . .

_____

_____

_____

_____

_____

If we are faithless, he remains faithful, for he cannot disown himself.
2 Timothy 2:13

Lord, I pray for the woman reading this right now who **can't seem to catch a break**. Her heart is weary, and she is struggling to see Your goodness. Give her strength, Lord. You see her, and You love her so very much. Help her not to draw conclusions about Your love based on her circumstances. Show her Your favor and be merciful to her as she seeks to honor You in this difficult season. Cover her with Your grace and Your comfort tonight, Lord. Amen.

Lord, even though I don't understand, I will . . .

———————————————————————————

———————————————————————————

———————————————————————————

———————————————————————————

Do not withhold your mercy from me, LORD; may your love and faithfulness always protect me.

Psalm 40:11

Lord, I pray for the woman reading this right now who **is struggling to find a friend she can trust.** She feels so alone and wishes she had someone to lean on. Secure her, satisfy her, and teach her first and foremost that she is treasured by You, Lord. You are right there with her. Bless her with that one friend she can depend on and empower her with the desire to love more than she desires to be loved (Proverbs 18:24). Overwhelm her with Your love tonight as she finds friendship in You first, Lord. Amen.

Lord, in my loneliness, help me to first focus on loving others by . . .

_____

_____

_____

_____

One who has unreliable friends soon comes to ruin, but there is a friend who sticks closer than a brother.

Proverbs 18:24

Lord, I pray for the woman reading this right now who **is struggling to get through each day**. She feels alone, and she needs to know You are beside her. Pour out Your love in her and through her. Help her to be obedient to what is right in front of her. Remind her that You are within her and that she will not fall (Psalm 46:5). Give her grace to see the meaning in the ordinary and unseen moments of her day as she trusts You, Lord. Amen.

Lord, with great love, help me to . . .

_____

_____

_____

_____

_____

God is within her, she will not fall; God will help her at break of day.

Psalm 46:5

night
74

Lord, I pray for the woman reading this right now who **finally feels settled for the first time in a long while.** Although things aren't perfect, she is grateful for this season. Help her to rest in Your goodness and kindness during this time and continue to show Your heart of love toward her. Fill her to overflowing as she rests in You. Continue to give her joy and hope for today and tomorrow, Lord. Amen.

Lord, in this season of rest, I thank You for . . .

_____

_____

_____

_____

_____

Praise the LORD. Give thanks to the LORD, for he is good; his love endures forever.

Psalm 106:1

Lord, I pray for the woman reading this right now who **feels she has been abandoned.** Show her You have not forgotten her. Surround her with Your love. Draw near to her and soothe her with the assurance that You know what she is walking through. She is not alone because You are with her always, to the end of the age (Matthew 28:20). Be her strength and her support as she leans on You, Lord. Amen.

Lord, because You know what it is like to feel abandoned, I will . . .

_____

_____

_____

_____

_____

And surely I am with you always, to the very end of the age.

Matthew 28:20

night
76

Lord, I pray for the woman reading this right now who **lacks the confidence to move forward with what You have for her.** Pour out Your Spirit and give her boldness, Lord. Take away her fear or insecurity. Help her to walk in the grace You give her so she can do what You are calling her to do. Go before her and provide all that she needs. Give her faith where she lacks faith and be beside her, Lord. Amen.

Lord, I will not fear because I know . . .

_____

_____

_____

_____

_____

So we say with confidence, "The Lord is my helper; I will not be afraid. What can mere mortals do to me?"

Hebrews 13:6

Lord, I pray for the woman reading this right now who **is struggling with insecurity**. Remind her of the real source of her worth and value, and of her identity. May Your love be her center, her anchor, and her foundation. Strengthen her by Your Spirit so that she has a deep and abiding confidence in who You are and who You have created her to be (Ephesians 3:16–18). She is a treasured gift, and she can rest securely in You tonight, Lord. Amen.

Lord, help me to see myself as You see me so I can . . .

_____

_____

_____

I pray that out of his glorious riches he may strengthen you with power through his Spirit. . . . And I pray that you, being rooted and established in love, may . . . grasp how wide and long and high and deep is the love of Christ.

Ephesians 3:16–18

night
78

Lord, I pray for the woman reading this right now who **is filled with dread at what is to come.** She is afraid and overwhelmed by all of the unknowns. Be a shield around her, Lord. Remind her that You go before her, and You sustain her in all things by Your grace (Deuteronomy 31:8). The future is Yours, and she has no reason to fear. Wrap her in Your embrace and be so near to her tonight, Lord. Amen.

Lord, because of who You are, I will not fear . . .

_____

_____

_____

_____

_____

The Lord himself goes before you and will be with you; he will never leave you nor forsake you. Do not be afraid; do not be discouraged.

Deuteronomy 31:8

Lord, I pray for the woman reading this right now who **feels unmotivated to do anything**. Renew her strength and refresh her faith tonight. Help her to see the gifts You have placed in her to be used for Your glory. She can walk with purpose and motivation when she walks closely with You. Fill her with Your Spirit and compel her by Your love to begin again with a new and greater sense of joy, Lord. Amen.

Lord, in faith, hope, and love, I will begin to . . .

_____

_____

_____

_____

Therefore, my dear brothers and sisters, stand firm. Let nothing move you. Always give yourselves fully to the work of the Lord, because you know that your labor in the Lord is not in vain.

1 Corinthians 15:58

Lord, I pray for the woman reading this right now who **feels uneasy**. She can't seem to put her finger on it, but things just seem off. Give her wisdom and help her to cling to You as she walks through this season. Fill her with courage and give her eyes to see what is from You and what may be from the enemy. Surround her with Your protection and care, and help her to sleep peacefully tonight, Lord. Amen.

Lord, I believe Your Spirit is telling me to . . .

_____

_____

_____

_____

_____

*I lie down and sleep; I wake again, because the L*ORD *sustains me.*

Psalm 3:5

night
81

Lord, I pray for the woman reading this right now who **needs direction**. She is at a crossroads, and she isn't sure which way to go. Help her to be patient in the waiting. Direct her steps and give her wisdom to walk according to Your will (Isaiah 30:21). Give her eyes to see what You have for her right where she is, and help her be faithful first in that place. Calm her heart and be near to her as she seeks answers, Lord. Amen.

Lord, I desire to be obedient to You by . . .

_____

_____

_____

_____

_____

Whether you turn to the right or to the left, your ears will hear a voice behind you, saying, "This is the way; walk in it."

Isaiah 30:21

night
82

Lord, I pray for the woman reading this right now who **feels numb inside.** She has been through so much and wonders if she'll ever feel alive again. Awaken her heart, Lord. Renew her desires and mind and will to follow You. Protect her from the enemy. You are a shield around her and the lifter of her head (Psalm 3:3). Surround her and give her grace to grow in love for You and others. Lift her spirits with Your love tonight, Lord. Amen.

Lord, awaken my heart once again for . . .

_____

_____

_____

_____

But you, Lord, are a shield around me, my glory, the One who lifts my head high.

Psalm 3:3

Lord, I pray for the woman reading this right now who **is struggling to trust You with her future**. Give her courage to place her plans in Your hands (Proverbs 16:3). Remind her that she won't always feel like she is wandering, Lord. You will reveal what You have for her. Your will and Your way are so much better than she can imagine, and she can rest in Your care for her. Be so near to her and alleviate the worry she feels tonight, Lord. Amen.

Lord, as I wait on You, I will . . .

_____

_____

_____

_____

_____

Commit to the LORD whatever you do, and he will establish your plans.

Proverbs 16:3

night
84

Lord, I pray for the woman reading this right now who **is tired of all the sleepless nights**. She tosses and turns. She is worn out from the day behind her but worried about the day ahead of her. Settle her thoughts and calm her heart (Matthew 11:28). Remind her that You have it all under Your control. She can trust You. Pour out Your peace on her so she can rest securely tonight, Lord. Amen.

Lord, when worry begins to invade, I will . . .

_____

_____

_____

_____

_____

Come to me, all you who are weary and burdened, and I will give you rest.

Matthew 11:28

night
85

Lord, I pray for the woman reading this right now who **is frustrated and wondering if she has been wasting time in this place.** She wants to get out or just move on. Show her that where You have her is not a wasted place or wasted time. There is a reason and a purpose. Help her to resist wanting to rush this season or these circumstances. Instead, enable her to run to You in dependence and trust. Cover her with Your grace and give her hope tonight, Lord. Amen.

Lord, help me not to rush this season by . . .

_____

_____

_____

_____

_____

He has made everything beautiful in its time.

Ecclesiastes 3:11

Lord, I pray for the woman reading this right now who **has lost her faith**. She is struggling to believe that You are even there. Pour out Your Spirit in a fresh way tonight. Help her to see that You are inviting her to go deeper. In the absence of her feelings, You are maturing her faith. You are growing trust and humility and greater dependence on You. Renew her confidence in You as she comes humbly to You, Lord. Amen.

Lord, even when You feel far away, I will . . .

_____

_____

_____

_____

Truly I tell you, if you have faith as small as a mustard seed, you can say to this mountain, "Move from here to there," and it will move. Nothing will be impossible for you.

Matthew 17:20

Lord, I pray for the woman reading this right now who **feels like giving up**. She is tired and exhausted and wonders what the point of this life is. Help her find the courage to reach out for help. Refresh her heart and mind and open her eyes to what matters most. Even when it is hard, enable her to endure because of what You have promised. In this world she will have trouble, but she can take heart because You have overcome (John 16:33). Give her power to follow You, faithfully and fully, Lord. Amen.

Lord, I will not give up because I know . . .

_____

_____

_____

_____

I have told you these things, so that in me you may have peace. In this world you will have trouble. But take heart! I have overcome the world.

John 16:33

night
88

Lord, I pray for the woman reading this right now who **has been betrayed**. Be with her right now in her pain and weeping, Lord. Remind her that You, Jesus, know what she is feeling. You too have experienced what she is enduring. Help her to give her pain to You. Heal her, soothe her wounds, and give her the strength to take another step. May Your grace be more than enough for her, Lord. Amen.

Lord, in my suffering, I ask You to . . .

_____

_____

_____

_____

_____

Praise be to the God and Father of our Lord Jesus Christ, the Father of compassion and the God of all comfort, who comforts us in all our troubles.

2 Corinthians 1:3–4

Lord, I pray for the woman reading this right now who **has been let down so many times that she is struggling to believe in the good and have hope again.** Guard her heart against growing colder and harder. Instead, soften her heart and restore the joy she once had. Give her new energy and enthusiasm to love You and those around her. Grow her faith through this season as she draws near to You, Lord. Amen.

Lord, soften my heart toward . . .

As for me, I call to God, and the LORD saves me. Evening, morning and noon I cry out in distress, and he hears my voice.

Psalm 55:16–17

night
90

Lord, I pray for the woman reading this right now who **feels disoriented by all she is walking through.** Strengthen her inner being with power and give her peace. When our world is spinning it can be hard to hold on to one thing. Help her to see what is most important or urgent right now and fill her with Your Spirit to pursue You above all else. Give her the sacredness of Your peaceful presence tonight, Lord. Amen.

Lord, even with everything going on, I will continue to . . .

_____

_____

_____

_____

Let the morning bring me word of your unfailing love, for I have put my trust in you. Show me the way I should go, for to you I entrust my life.

Psalm 143:8

Lord, I pray for the woman reading this right now who **is struggling with contentment**. Guard her heart against looking at what she doesn't have and thinks she needs. Instead, help her to focus on all she *does* have. May her life be rooted and overflowing with thankfulness (Colossians 2:7). Give her a grateful heart that is increasingly being filled with who You are and eyes to see Your goodness in her life, Lord. Amen.

Lord, instead of looking at what I don't have, I give You thanks for . . .

_____

_____

_____

_____

Rooted and built up in him, strengthened in the faith as you were taught, and overflowing with thankfulness.

Colossians 2:7

Lord, I pray for the woman reading this right now who **feels worn and weary**. She needs You, Lord. Remind her that You are with her, and You are for her. Give her the grace to endure so that, in time, she will experience the fruit of pressing on in this hard season. She will reap a harvest of blessing if she doesn't give up (Galatians 6:9). Renew her faith and refresh her strength, Lord. Amen.

Lord, I will carry on in the area of my . . .

_____

_____

_____

_____

_____

Let us not become weary in doing good, for at the proper time we will reap a harvest if we do not give up.

Galatians 6:9

Lord, I pray for the woman reading this right now who **is doubting Your love for her.** Help her to look to the cross (1 John 4:9–10). Give her eyes to see the costly and sacrificial love of Jesus for her. Protect her from the enemy, who wants her to doubt and be discouraged. Even when she doesn't feel it, remind her of Your loyal and steadfast love toward her. Cover her with Your grace and be so near to her tonight, Lord. Amen.

Lord, I know You love me because . . .

_____

_____

_____

_____

This is how God showed his love among us: He sent his one and only Son into the world that we might live through him. This is love: not that we loved God, but that he loved us and sent his Son as an atoning sacrifice for our sins.

1 John 4:9–10

Lord, I pray for the woman reading this right now who **needs a reminder that there is always hope when she stays close to You.** Surround her and protect her from the enemy who wants to discourage and even destroy all that You are doing in her life. Give her the gift of faith through Your Spirit. There are new seasons and new circumstances ahead of her if she doesn't give up. Help her to walk with You and lean on You, Lord. Amen.

Lord, with Your help, I will not lose hope in . . .

_____

_____

_____

_____

_____

The Lord is near to all who call on him, to all who call on him in truth.

Psalm 145:18

Lord, I pray for the woman reading this right now who **has been hurt by someone she trusted**. Comfort her and soothe her as she brings her pain and sorrow to You. But help her not to stay there in that painful place. In time, bring healing and hope and forgiveness. You know what she is feeling, Jesus. Give her the strength to trust again. Draw near to her as she draws near to You tonight, Lord. Amen.

> *Lord, You know what it feels like to be forsaken.*
> *I give over to You the hurt of . . .*

Even if my father and mother abandon me, the LORD will hold me close.

Psalm 27:10 NLT

night
96

Lord, I pray for the woman reading this right now who **wonders if You hear her prayers**. Remind her that You do. You turn Your heart toward her as You turn Your ears toward her. She is not alone. You are faithful and loyal even to a thousand generations (Deuteronomy 7:9). Give her the faith to believe that You love her by listening to her, Lord. Amen.

Lord, I know You hear me, so I will not stop . . .

Know therefore that the LORD your God is God; he is the faithful God, keeping his covenant of love to a thousand generations of those who love him and keep his commandments.

Deuteronomy 7:9

Lord, I pray for the woman reading this right now who **has finally found her courage**. Give her the wisdom and strength to do what You are asking her to do. Guide her steps and remove any obstacles that stand in her way. Lead her to do what You are calling her to do with love and humility. Remind her that You go with her, behind her, and on every side of her in all that she does. Help her to trust You, Lord. Amen.

Lord, with Your help, I will take the next step to . . .

_____

_____

_____

_____

_____

Finally, be strong in the Lord and in his mighty power.

Ephesians 6:10

night
98

Lord, I pray for the woman reading this right now who **is stuck in a cycle of sin**. Remind her that You love her, but by Your grace, help her to see the life You want for her. Lovingly convict her and soften her heart. Lead her out of sin to rest in You, Jesus, as her Savior and Redeemer. You are the One who restores us when we fall. Give her a new heart to want to honor You more than anything. Cover her with Your grace as she comes to You tonight, Lord. Amen.

Lord, I confess and turn from the sin of . . .

_____

_____

_____

_____

Repent, then, and turn to God, so that your sins may be wiped out, that times of refreshing may come from the Lord.

Acts 3:19

Lord, I pray for the woman reading this right now who **has lost her joy**. Give her understanding and show her why her ultimate hope is found in You. Help her to pray as King David did, "restore to me the joy of your salvation" (Psalm 51:12). Pour out Your Spirit in a fresh way and give her a new hunger for You. Remind her that You are the only true and lasting source of joy. Fill her heart with hope tonight, Lord. Amen.

Lord, I sense that I have lost my joy because of . . .

_____

_____

_____

_____

Restore to me the joy of your salvation and grant me a willing spirit, to sustain me.

Psalm 51:12

Lord, I pray for the woman reading this right now who **is struggling in a relationship with a loved one.** Give her wisdom on how to take the next step. I pray for peace and a willingness to reconcile. Help her to have a heart that is humble and seeking to understand. Fill her with Your love and bring a new and deeper relationship out of the one that is currently broken. Restore peace and heal what has been hurt, Lord. Amen.

Lord, in humility, I will take the next step of . . .

_____

_____

_____

_____

Bear with each other and forgive one another if any of you has a grievance against someone. Forgive as the Lord forgave you.

Colossians 3:13

101

Lord, I pray for the woman reading this right now who **needs assurance that You are for her**. Give her eyes to see Your presence and provision (Psalm 37:25). Speak to her through Your Word. And even when she struggles to feel Your presence, help her to walk in obedience to what she knows is true and right. Be kind to her. Show her Your mercy and be close to her as she longs to know You are there, Lord. Amen.

Lord, I know You are with me because . . .

_____

_____

_____

_____

I was young and now I am old, yet I have never seen the righteous forsaken or their children begging bread.

Psalm 37:25

night
102

Lord, I pray for the woman reading this right now who **feels no one sees who she is or what she has done**. Remind her that her true worth is found in You and not in what others think of her. You know her and the motivations of her heart completely. That is all that matters. She can be at peace because You have called her Your child (1 John 3:1). Speak to her and comfort her tonight, Lord. Amen.

Lord, I know You see my . . .

_____

_____

_____

_____

_____

See what great love the Father has lavished on us, that we should be called children of God! And that is what we are!

1 John 3:1

Lord, I pray for the woman reading this right now who **is cautiously looking forward to what is to come.** Give her joy and remind her that Your heart is good (Psalm 145:9). You desire to bless her and show her Your favor. Fill her with faith and hopefulness about what is to come. Be near to her as she trusts You with the days ahead, Lord. Amen.

Lord, it is with confidence that I believe You will . . .

_____

_____

_____

_____

_____

_____

The Lord is good to all; he has compassion on all he has made.

Psalm 145:9

Lord, I pray for the woman reading this right now who **wonders how You could let this happen to her.** She trusted that You would intervene and come through for her, but she feels her prayers weren't answered. She is broken. Comfort her in this moment, Lord. Guard her heart against becoming hard. Give her the faith to release what she is walking through, to surrender it to You, knowing that You see her, and You love her. Help her to trust You, Lord. Amen.

Lord, even though I don't understand, I will trust You with . . .

_____

_____

_____

_____

Naked I came from my mother's womb, and naked I will depart. The Lord gave and the Lord has taken away; may the name of the Lord be praised.

Job 1:21

Lord, I pray for the woman reading this right now who **is hoping for better days to come.** Help her not to grow weary, discouraged, or distracted by what "could happen." Fill her with Your Spirit so she might remain hopeful and joyful in the midst of the hard stuff she is facing. Keep Your promises to her as she perseveres and holds on to hope that You will come through for her, Lord. Amen.

Lord, I am trusting You that one day You will . . .

_____

_____

_____

_____

_____

The LORD will keep you from all harm—he will watch over your life; the LORD will watch over your coming and going both now and forevermore.

Psalm 121:7–8

night
106

Lord, I pray for the woman reading this right now who **feels disorganized.** She is running in a million different directions, and she can't keep it together. Bring clarity out of her confusion. Give her perspective and show her what matters most right now. Help her to focus on being faithful to what You would have for her in this season. Overwhelm her with Your peace tonight, Lord. Amen.

Lord, no matter what is going on around me, I will keep my eyes on . . .

_____

_____

_____

_____

_____

For God is not a God of disorder but of peace.

1 Corinthians 14:33

Lord, I pray for the woman reading this right now who **feels uncomfortable with her circumstances**. She is worried and unsure about the future. Give her peace, Lord. Help her to give her attention to what is right in front of her. Open her eyes to where You are leading and give her confidence that You will not let her walk alone. Strengthen her as she follows Your will and way, Lord. Amen.

Lord, I will keep being faithful with . . .

_____

_____

_____

_____

_____

For he guards the course of the just and protects the way of his faithful ones.

Proverbs 2:8

Lord, I pray for the woman reading this right now who **wishes You would answer her prayers**. She has waited for You to come through, and she wonders if You are listening. Hear her prayers. Answer them and show her Your goodness. She can be confident that You who began a good work will bring it to completion (Philippians 1:6). Give her faith as she waits on Your provision and Your timing, and help her to be faithful in the waiting, Lord. Amen.

Lord, I am trusting that You will hear my prayer for . . .

_____

_____

_____

_____

Being confident of this, that he who began a good work in you will carry it on to completion until the day of Christ Jesus.

Philippians 1:6

Lord, I pray for the woman reading this right now who **is in danger of quitting too soon.** Refresh the dreams that she once had and help her not to give up on the plan and purpose You have for her. Remind her that there is fruit in enduring. Honor her faithfulness and give her a new heart to hunger and thirst after You. Renew her strength and give her hope tonight, Lord. Amen.

Lord, when I want to quit, give me the strength to endure . . .

_____

_____

_____

_____

Blessed is the one who perseveres under trial because, having stood the test, that person will receive the crown of life that the Lord has promised to those who love him.

James 1:12

Lord, I pray for the woman reading this right now who **is doubting You will show up for her in her hard situation.** She is struggling to trust Your faithfulness. Pour out Your kindness and show her Your goodness. Answer her prayers as she waits on You. Guard her heart against discouragement and doubt (Psalm 27:14). Teach her to desire Your will above all. Remind her that You are with her and be so near to her tonight, Lord. Amen.

Lord, I will not give up as I wait for You to . . .

_____

_____

_____

_____

_____

Wait for the Lord; be strong and take heart and wait for the Lord.

Psalm 27:14

night
111

Lord, I pray for the woman reading this right now who **is sick and tired of being sick and tired**. She needs Your hope tonight, Lord. Turn her eyes to You. Remind her of Your grace and Your love for her. Give her the rest You promise (Psalm 62:1). More than just getting through, give her more of You. She needs Your refreshment. Pour out Your Spirit on her tonight, Lord. Amen.

Lord, I need Your Spirit to continue . . .

_____

_____

_____

_____

_____

Truly my soul finds rest in God; my salvation comes from him.

Psalm 62:1

night
112

Lord, I pray for the woman reading this right now who **is struggling to discern Your voice.** She is seeking direction from You, and she feels so confused. Give her ears to hear You, Lord. Guard her against discouragement and the lies of the enemy. Speak to her about what she needs to hear most right now, and with clarity. Be her Light in the darkness. Show her the way, Your way, Lord. Amen.

Lord, with clarity, would You speak to me about . . .

_____

_____

_____

_____

_____

Come quickly to help me, my Lord and my Savior.

Psalm 38:22

Lord, I pray for the woman reading this right now who **is feeling hopeful**. Although things aren't perfect, she is starting to see a break in the clouds. Continue to go before her and provide for her, Lord. Open doors and bring the change she needs. Give her hope and release her to walk into the future with confidence and expectation. Cover her with Your lovingkindness as she trusts in You, Lord. Amen.

Lord, help me to trust You and be hopeful for . . .

_____

_____

_____

_____

_____

I waited patiently for the Lord; he turned to me and heard my cry.

Psalm 40:1

Lord, I pray for the woman reading this right now who **needs to remember that who she is becoming is more important than what she is doing.** She hates feeling unproductive, so she goes and goes and goes. Give her rest, Lord. Draw her close to You and pour out Your love through Your Spirit. Help her to trust that You are working in her and through her and that everything does not depend on her—it is You, Lord, who is in control. May she surrender to You and find peace in You tonight, Lord. Amen.

Lord, help me to surrender . . .

_____

_____

_____

_____

Come with me by yourselves to a quiet place and get some rest.

Mark 6:31

Lord, I pray for the woman reading this right now who **can't imagine how things will get better.** She wants to believe You will show up, but she is struggling to see Your hand in her life right now. Guard her against despair, Lord. Protect her against the lies of the enemy. Remind her that You can make all things new. You *do* make all things new (Revelation 21:5). Nothing is impossible or too hard for You. Fight for her as she looks to You for help tonight, Lord. Amen.

Lord, I know nothing is too hard for You, so I give You . . .

_____

_____

_____

_____

He who was seated on the throne said, "I am making everything new!"
Then he said, "Write this down, for these words are trustworthy and true."

Revelation 21:5

night
116

Lord, I pray for the woman reading this right now who **is struggling with chronic sickness**. Bring relief in her pain, Lord. Give her the grace to do what she can but also to surrender the rest to Your power and care. Heal her and restore her (Jeremiah 17:14). Empower her to love You even in her suffering and believe that You will use this for Your glory. Overwhelm her with Your peace and hope tonight, Lord. Amen.

Lord, I will love You in my sickness by . . .

_____

_____

_____

_____

_____

Heal me, Lᴏʀᴅ, and I will be healed; save me and I will be saved, for you are the one I praise.

Jeremiah 17:14

night
117

Lord, I pray for the woman reading this right now who **is unsatisfied with where she is at in her life.** She thought she'd be in a different place by now, but it seems like nothing ever goes her way. Help her to surrender her desires to You and seek Your will and way. Give her eyes to see the good things in her life. Be with her in the moments she questions You and show her that You are there leading her, Lord. Amen.

Lord, teach me to be content with . . .

_____

_____

_____

_____

_____

All my longings lie open before you, Lord; my sighing is not hidden from you.

Psalm 38:9

night
118

Lord, I pray for the woman reading this right now who **feels unloved.** She feels so unwanted and alone. Show her Your grace and pour out Your love in her heart through Your Spirit. Help her to hear Your voice, reminding her that she is loved by You. Give her eyes to see You, Jesus, and the outpouring of Your love for her on the cross (John 15:13). Be so near to her tonight, Lord. Amen.

Lord, even when I don't feel loved, I know that I am because . . .

_____

_____

_____

_____

_____

Greater love has no one than this: to lay down one's life for one's friends.

John 15:13

Lord, I pray for the woman reading this right now who **feels her life is chaotic and unmanageable.** She wishes she could just get it together, Lord. Help her to find peace and learn to rest in You. Calm her and reassure her that You have it together, Lord. She can count on You and look to You to work through her whether she has it all together or not (2 Corinthians 12:9). You are in complete control. Remind her to lean on You for her strength when she is tempted to do it all alone. She can walk securely in Your care, comforted by Your grace for her, Lord. Amen.

Lord, I know that I don't need to "get it all together" because . . .

_____

_____

_____

But he said to me, "My grace is sufficient for you, for my power is made perfect in weakness." Therefore I will boast all the more gladly about my weaknesses, so that Christ's power may rest on me.

2 Corinthians 12:9

night
120

Lord, I pray for the woman reading this right now who **feels unworthy**. Remind her of what is true no matter how she feels. She is fearfully and wonderfully made (Psalm 139:14). Help her to understand that she is full of dignity and beauty—and worth. Flood her with Your love and give her the confidence to walk securely as Your beloved child, Lord. Amen.

Lord, I am not worthy because of what I do, but because . . .

_____

_____

_____

_____

_____

I praise you because I am fearfully and wonderfully made; your works are wonderful, I know that full well.

Psalm 139:14

Lord, I pray for the woman reading this right now who **is mourning**. Come close to her as she offers You her sorrow. Soothe her and alleviate the heaviness she feels. Help her to feel the pain without being consumed by it, and bring healing. Take the hurt and turn it into a new hope (Psalm 30:11). Transform it into a deeper hope in You. Be so very close to her tonight as she cries out to You, Lord. Amen.

Lord, in faith and hope, I offer You the pain of . . .

_____

_____

_____

_____

_____

You turned my wailing into dancing; you removed my sackcloth and clothed me with joy.

Psalm 30:11

Lord, I pray for the woman reading this right now who **feels she is running out of time.** She feels she has wasted so much of her life focusing on the things that didn't really matter. Help her to let go of the past and not be troubled by the future. Shift her focus to You right now. It is never too late to be used by You (1 Peter 4:1–2). Give her the wisdom to live today faithfully and fully for You and those around her, Lord. Amen.

Lord, it is never too late to follow You, so starting today I will . . .

_____

_____

_____

Therefore, since Christ suffered in his body, arm yourselves also with the same attitude, because whoever suffers in the body is done with sin. As a result, they do not live the rest of their earthly lives for evil human desires, but rather for the will of God.

1 Peter 4:1–2

Lord, I pray for the woman reading this right now who **feels apathetic**. She wishes she cared more about the way she spends her days, but she doesn't. Out of Your kindness, wake her up spiritually. Renew in her the joy of her salvation (Psalm 35:9). Restore a new sense of urgency to love You and serve You. Where there is sin that might be causing her heart to harden, bring conviction and confession. Shower her with the sweetness of Your forgiveness tonight, Lord. Amen.

Lord, I confess that my heart may be apathetic because . . .

_____

_____

_____

_____

_____

Then my soul will rejoice in the Lord and delight in his salvation.

Psalm 35:9

night
124

Lord, I pray for the woman reading this right now who **desires to be poor in spirit** (Matthew 5:3). By Your grace, help her to see who she really is—a loved sinner. Root out any pride and grow within her a heart that is truly humble and dependent on You. Remind her that You alone are God and that the fruit that lasts comes from Your working through her. Be near to her as she humbly turns to You, Lord. Amen.

Lord, give me humility in the area of . . .

_____

_____

_____

_____

_____

Blessed are the poor in spirit, for theirs is the kingdom of heaven.

Matthew 5:3

Lord, I pray for the woman reading this right now who **feels persecuted by those around her**. She feels like an outsider in her walk with You. Surround her like a shield. Be her refuge and remind her that she is not alone. Give her compassion for those around her who may not understand her faith, but also give her courage to live boldly for You. Help her to remember that pleasing You is most important (1 Thessalonians 2:4). She can walk securely as Your child, Lord. Amen.

Lord, I will keep being faithful with my . . .

_____

_____

_____

_____

On the contrary, we speak as those approved by God to be entrusted with the gospel. We are not trying to please people but God, who tests our hearts.

1 Thessalonians 2:4

night
126

Lord, I pray for the woman reading this right now who **wonders if her life will ever be normal again.** She is struggling with all that has come her way, and she doesn't know how to move on. Help her to release what she has walked through to You, Lord. Guard her mind against wanting to go back or fearing what is ahead. Enable her to accept what is before her with resilience. Teach her to walk in faith, hope, and love. Above all, give her the power to live for You today, Lord. Amen.

Lord, I release . . .

_____

_____

_____

_____

_____

Be pleased to save me, Lord; come quickly, Lord, to help me.

Psalm 40:13

Lord, I pray for the woman reading this right now who **can't see a clear path ahead**. Teach her that she doesn't have to see clearly. All she needs to do is follow You, Jesus. You are the Light of the world. Whoever follows You never walks in darkness (John 8:12). Help her to trust You, one step at a time. You are the One who is leading her and sees the future with perfect clarity (Isaiah 46:10). Help her to hold on to that truth tonight, Lord. Amen.

Lord, even though I can't see how . . .

I make known the end from the beginning, from ancient times, what is still to come.

Isaiah 46:10

night
128

Lord, I pray for the woman reading this right now who **feels distracted**. Carve out of her busy and crazy life the things she needs to focus on now. Help her to see with clarity and resolve. Eliminate all the things that are taking her away from what matters most—the things that are keeping her from loving You and loving others as she should. Be her anchor as she focuses her heart and mind on You, Lord. Amen.

Lord, in order to love You and others better,
I will prayerfully focus on . . .

_____

_____

_____

_____

_____

But my eyes are fixed on you, Sovereign LORD; in you I take refuge.

Psalm 141:8

Lord, I pray for the woman reading this right now who **is in a funk**. Open her eyes to see why she feels this way. Give her grace to get up, to keep going, no matter how she feels. Teach her endurance and faithfulness. Help her to fix her eyes on You, Jesus, who persevered out of love and obedience (Hebrews 12:2). Remove this funk and replace it with a new hunger and thirst for You, Lord. Amen.

Lord, give me the grace to keep being faithful in . . .

_____

_____

_____

_____

_____

I can do all this through him who gives me strength.

Philippians 4:13

night
130

Lord, I pray for the woman reading this right now who **feels forgotten**. In her pain of feeling alone, protect her from becoming consumed with how she feels. You have not forgotten her, Lord, and You never will (Isaiah 49:15–16). Enable her to shift her feelings of being forgotten into an offering of love to You and others. Turn her eyes away from herself and toward Your grace and mercy in her life. Help her to lean wholly on You for her peace, Lord. Amen.

Lord, instead of focusing on feeling forgotten, I will find peace in . . .

_____

_____

_____

_____

Can a mother forget the baby at her breast and have no compassion on the child she has borne? Though she may forget, I will not forget you! See, I have engraved you on the palms of my hands; your walls are ever before me.

Isaiah 49:15–16

Lord, I pray for the woman reading this right now who **is ready for a change**. As You prepare her for what may be next, give her patience. Teach her during this season to lean completely on You. As tempting as it might be, help her not to get ahead of You but give her the wisdom to wait on You. You are working out Your will in her life (Philippians 2:13). Go before her and open the doors for her as she seeks to follow You. Bring the change she is hoping for, Lord. Amen.

Lord, as I wait on You, in Your kindness, bring change to . . .

_____

_____

_____

_____

For it is God who works in you to will and to act in order to fulfill his good purpose.

Philippians 2:13

Lord, I pray for the woman reading this right now who **wishes she had friends**. She feels so alone and wishes there was someone she could lean on. In this season of loneliness, draw near to her. Be her faithful companion and help her to cultivate greater intimacy with You. Give her the courage to take a step to create the kind of friendship she is longing for. There is someone who needs a friend just like she does. Help her to find that friend she is longing for, Lord. Amen.

Lord, give me the wisdom to take a step toward friendship by . . .

_____

_____

_____

_____

I no longer call you servants, because a servant does not know his master's business. Instead, I have called you friends, for everything that I learned from my Father I have made known to you.

John 15:15

Lord, I pray for the woman reading this right now who **needs hope**. Fill her with confidence in who You are. Remind her that her hope is anchored in Your character and not in her circumstances. Show her Your faithfulness and help her to fix her eyes on You, Jesus. You are the One who, by Your death and resurrection, has given us a living hope that cannot spoil, fade, or perish (1 Peter 1:3–4). She can rest in that truth tonight, Lord. Amen.

Lord, give me hope in the area of my . . .

_____

_____

_____

_____

In his great mercy he has given us new birth into a living hope through the resurrection of Jesus Christ from the dead, and into an inheritance that can never perish, spoil or fade. This inheritance is kept in heaven for you.

1 Peter 1:3–4

night
134

Lord, I pray for the woman reading this right now who **feels unappreciated**. Remind her that her first love is You, and pleasing You is her first priority. You see her and appreciate her whether anyone else does or not. And You have promised that You reward her faithfulness that is done in secret when no one is watching or cheering her on (Matthew 6:6). Help her to be satisfied by Your loving gaze alone, Lord. Amen.

Lord, I will not be discouraged but will remain faithful in . . .

_____

_____

_____

_____

But when you pray, go into your room, close the door and pray to your Father, who is unseen. Then your Father, who sees what is done in secret, will reward you.

Matthew 6:6

Lord, I pray for the woman reading this right now who **is longing for peace.** She knows she should trust You, but her heart is unsettled. Help her to give You her present and her future. Guard her heart against worry and all that is happening now or could happen in the future. You will take care of her. Let her rest in Your faithfulness and have confidence that she is safe with You (Psalm 91:4). Be near to her tonight, Lord. Amen.

Lord, as I look at today and tomorrow, I rest in Your . . .

_____

_____

_____

_____

He will cover you with his feathers, and under his wings you will find refuge; his faithfulness will be your shield and rampart.

Psalm 91:4

night
136

Lord, I pray for the woman reading this right now who **wonders where You are**. Her life is so hard, and she wonders why You haven't shown up. Show Yourself to her, Lord. Give her the eyes of faith to see that You are with her and all the ways You are working, even in this hard season. She can trust that this season won't last forever (2 Corinthians 4:17–18). Help her to find hope in You tonight, Lord. Amen.

Lord, even when I can't see You, I will trust . . .

_____

_____

_____

_____

For our light and momentary troubles are achieving for us an eternal glory that far outweighs them all. So we fix our eyes not on what is seen, but on what is unseen, since what is seen is temporary, but what is unseen is eternal.

2 Corinthians 4:17–18

Lord, I pray for the woman reading this right now who **is longing for joy again**. Her heart feels heavy, and she wants relief. Fill her with Your Spirit. Only You bring true and lasting joy, so renew her joy—the joy that comes from walking with You and serving You. Weeping may last for the night, but joy does come in the morning (Psalm 30:5). Lighten the load she is carrying and bring expectation to her days, Lord. Amen.

Lord, renew the joy I once had in . . .

_____

_____

_____

_____

For his anger lasts only a moment, but his favor lasts a lifetime; weeping may stay for the night, but rejoicing comes in the morning.

Psalm 30:5

night
138

Lord, I pray for the woman reading this right now who **is struggling to find her purpose.** You have given her gifts to be used for Your glory. Lead her to use those gifts to serve You and those around her. Show her what You want for her and give her the courage to take a step toward serving You. She can find strength as she leans on You and trusts You to use her for Your glory, Lord. Amen.

Lord, I will take the next step toward Your purposes for me by . . .

_____

_____

_____

_____

_____

Be strong and take heart, all you who hope in the LORD.

Psalm 31:24

Lord, I pray for the woman reading this right now who **feels no one cares for her.** Silence the voice of the enemy in her heart and mind, Lord. Give her ears to hear Your voice—Your voice that calls her Your child. You are her Father. Help her to live out of Your love and stay rooted in what is most true of her. You will take care of her. She can trust You, Lord. Amen.

Lord, the truest thing about me is that I am . . .

_____

_____

_____

_____

_____

Hear, Lord, and be merciful to me; Lord, be my help.

Psalm 30:10

night
140

Lord, I pray for the woman reading this right now who **is waiting for You to come through for her**. She wonders if you will ever answer her prayers. Help her to surrender to You in this season. Don't let her be discouraged as she waits. Prevent her from just rushing through these circumstances. You can use the waiting in her life. Draw close to her and turn her waiting into worship, Lord. Amen.

Lord, as I wait for You to answer, help me to . . .

_____

_____

_____

_____

_____

But you, Lord, do not be far from me. You are my strength; come quickly to help me.

Psalm 22:19

Lord, I pray for the woman reading this right now who **is ready to throw in the towel**. She can't imagine how she can go on. Lord, give her the grace to keep going even when she wants to give up. Don't let her just accept her circumstances but help her to embrace them with the hope that You are faithful through it all. Remind her that there is fruit to come if she doesn't quit—a harvest really is possible. Be so very near to her tonight as she clings to You, Lord. Amen.

Lord, give me faith and hope to keep going and trust You for . . .

_____

_____

_____

_____

In my distress I called to the LORD; I cried to my God for help. From his temple he heard my voice; my cry came before him, into his ears.

Psalm 18:6

Lord, I pray for the woman reading this right now who **always wakes at 3 a.m.** Take captive her thoughts. Help her to stop replaying the past. Protect her from the fear of the future. Whatever movie reel of her life is playing over and over in her mind at that hour, remind her that You are the God who never sleeps. You are always watching over her and You won't let her go. Give her deep and satisfying rest (Proverbs 3:24) as she trusts in You, Lord. Amen.

Lord, help me to sleep soundly and stop thinking about . . .

_____

_____

_____

_____

When you lie down, you will not be afraid; when you lie down, your sleep will be sweet.

Proverbs 3:24

night
143

Lord, I pray for the woman reading this right now who **feels afraid**. Fill her mind with Your power and Your wisdom and Your goodness. Crowd out any anxious thoughts she is having and replace them with thoughts of who You are—sovereign and faithful. You see her, and You love her. Help her to trust that You will take care of her and turn her worry into worship tonight, Lord. Amen.

Lord, empower me not to be ruled by fear of . . .

_____

_____

_____

_____

Whoever dwells in the shelter of the Most High will rest in the shadow of the Almighty. I will say of the Lord, "He is my refuge and my fortress, my God, in whom I trust."

Psalm 91:1–2

Lord, I pray for the woman reading this right now who **can't seem to find her footing**. Give her wisdom to see the meaning and purpose of her life amid the unknowns. She feels unsure about so much in her life, but she can place those uncertainties in Your hands. Draw near to her as she draws near to You. Open her eyes to Your active presence in her life and help her to journey securely with You, Lord. Amen.

Lord, be my firm foundation by reminding me of . . .

_____

_____

_____

_____

_____

He will not let your foot slip—he who watches over you will not slumber.

Psalm 121:3

Lord, I pray for the woman reading this right now who **finally feels hopeful**. Give her greater permission to believe You have a heart for her good—a heart to bless her. Expose the places of her heart where she doubts Your kindness and generosity and help her to see that You want life for her. Continue to lift her spirits and give her the new season or circumstances she is looking forward to. Bring new life where she has needed it, Lord. Amen.

Lord, bring resurrection and new life to my . . .

_____

_____

_____

_____

_____

Sing to the Lord a new song, his praise from the ends of the earth.

Isaiah 42:10

Lord, I pray for the woman reading this right now who **feels trapped by her current circumstances**. She has been praying for a door to open and for relief from where she is, but You haven't moved yet. Don't let her be discouraged, Lord. Keep her from wanting to give up. Help her to hold on to You and to keep waiting for You and Your timing. She can trust You completely, Lord. Amen.

Lord, in Your timing, will You bring about change in . . .

_____

_____

_____

_____

_____

Though I walk in the midst of trouble, you preserve my life.

Psalm 138:7

Lord, I pray for the woman reading this right now who **wonders why life has to be so hard.** She is tired and weary from all the pain. Remind her of how You have loved her in Your suffering, Jesus. Give her the grace to love You back in her suffering. In her hard seasons, teach her faithfulness. Help her to keep her eyes fixed on You in this hard but holy season. Ease her burdens and be close to her tonight, Lord. Amen.

Lord, turn this hard season into a holy season by . . .

_____

_____

_____

_____

But you, Sovereign Lord, help me for your name's sake; out of the goodness of your love, deliver me.

Psalm 109:21

night
148

Lord, I pray for the woman reading this right now who **can't see the way forward.** She is struggling to know what is next. Open her eyes to see You and where You are leading more clearly. Give her faith and trust in You, the One who has promised to go before her. Even though she can't see the future, give her faith to believe that You are in control. Let that be enough for her to experience peace and joy tonight, Lord. Amen.

Lord, even though I can't see the future, I will . . .

_____

_____

_____

_____

The LORD himself goes before you and will be with you; he will never leave you nor forsake you. Do not be afraid; do not be discouraged.

Deuteronomy 31:8

Lord, I pray for the woman reading this right now who **has been wrongfully accused**. Please protect her and restore her reputation. Give her back what she feels she has lost. Uncover the truth and allow Your justice to show what is right. Prove her innocence, Lord. Help her to find peace as she surrenders outcomes to You and trusts You will take care of her, Lord. Amen.

Lord, help me to entrust myself to You by . . .

"No weapon forged against you will prevail, and you will refute every tongue that accuses you. This is the heritage of the servants of the LORD, and this is their vindication from me," declares the LORD.

Isaiah 54:17

night
150

Lord, I pray for the woman reading this right now who **feels she is always rushing.** She knows she needs to slow down, but she isn't sure how. Help her to rest in Your care for her and her circumstances. She doesn't need to hold everything together because You already are doing that. Open her eyes to the areas where she has taken on too much and give her wisdom to simplify her life. Assure her that she can trust You to take care of everything that concerns her, Lord. Amen.

Lord, show me how to slow down with . . .

_____

_____

_____

_____

_____

Though it linger, wait for it; it will certainly come and will not delay.

Habakkuk 2:3

night
151

Lord, I pray for the woman reading this right now who **is afraid of what is to come.** Comfort her with the truth that whatever the future holds, You will be there. She has nothing to fear. You will give her the strength and resilience to face each day as it comes. She does not have to fear because You've gone before her. Give her peace as she trusts in You and be so close to her in the moments she feels weak, Lord. Amen.

Lord, I give You the fear of . . .

_____

_____

_____

_____

_____

Hear my cry for help, my King and my God, for to you I pray.
Psalm 5:2

night
152

Lord, I pray for the woman reading this right now who **is trying to hear Your voice in the middle of the noise.** She so desperately wants to hear from You. Silence the voices that do not come from You, Lord. Eliminate distractions or desires that are not from You and tune her ear to Yours. Give her clarity so she can honor You in what You want for her. Speak to her and guide her tonight and always, Lord. Amen.

Lord, I need to hear Your voice speak to me about . . .

_____

_____

_____

_____

Call to me and I will answer you and tell you great and unsearchable things you do not know.

Jeremiah 33:3

Lord, I pray for the woman reading this right now who **needs strength**. In her weakness, sustain her and give her grace. Don't let her be overwhelmed by what is behind her or ahead of her. You have given her this moment. This day. You will provide what she needs now. Remind her that it is Your presence and power, Jesus, that give us everything we need. Fill her with Your power and be with her, Lord. Amen.

Lord, help me to rely on Your strength by . . .

_____

_____

_____

_____

_____

Hear my prayer, O God; listen to the words of my mouth.

Psalm 54:2

night
154

Lord, I pray for the woman reading this right now who **wants more for her life**. She is ready to give her whole life to You and Your plan. Create in her a heart that hungers for You. Satisfy her thirst for more with more of You. Give her wisdom for how she can move closer to You and help her to keep in step with Your Spirit (Galatians 5:25). Grow her faith and give her greater faithfulness in her life, Lord. Amen.

Lord, I will take the next step in my walk with You by . . .

_____

_____

_____

_____

_____

Since we live by the Spirit, let us keep in step with the Spirit.

Galatians 5:25

Lord, I pray for the woman reading this right now who **desires to be meek**. You are the true example of meekness (Matthew 11:29). You are strong and powerful. Yet in Your strength, You were never out of control. You did not try to control or manipulate. Help her to follow in Your footsteps and live by Your example. Empowering her by Your Spirit, help her to be kind and gentle, yet unmovable in what is true and right, Lord. Amen.

Lord, teach me to be meek in . . .

_____

_____

_____

_____

Take my yoke upon you and learn from me, for I am gentle and humble in heart, and you will find rest for your souls.

Matthew 11:29

night
156

Lord, I pray for the woman reading this right now who **is holding on to her faith in the middle of heartbreak.** Hold her so close during this time, Lord. Remind her that You are with her, and You are weeping with her. You know her struggle and her pain. With care and love, begin to piece her heart back together again. Make it whole. Sustain her and give her the gift of Your nearness tonight, Lord. Amen.

Lord, heal my heart from the pain of . . .

_____

_____

_____

_____

_____

Listen to my prayer, O God, do not ignore my plea; hear me and answer me. My thoughts trouble me and I am distraught.

Psalm 55:1–2

Lord, I pray for the woman reading this right now who **is tired of feeling stuck**. Help her to see that being stuck is not always bad. Give her eyes to see where and how You are calling her deeper during this time. Show her how feeling stuck is an opportunity for new growth and greater intimacy with You. In the waiting, You are working. Help her to trust that Your plan is good, Lord. Amen.

Lord, help me to trust You are moving even though I feel . . .

_____

_____

_____

_____

_____

He lifted me out of the slimy pit, out of the mud and mire; he set my feet on a rock and gave me a firm place to stand.

Psalm 40:2

night
158

Lord, I pray for the woman reading this right now who **needs peace**. Surround her with Your presence. Wrap Your arms around her and protect her from fear or worry. Remind her that she is not alone and that You are right there beside her. You go before her and behind her and on every side. She can be at peace because You love her, and You are fighting for her. Be so near to her as she finds her strength in You, Lord. Amen.

Lord, help me to find peace in You and to stop . . .

_____

_____

_____

_____

_____

For he himself is our peace.
Ephesians 2:14

Lord, I pray for the woman reading this right now who **needs to be loved**. She feels alone and unwanted. Satisfy her deepest longings, Lord. Quench her thirst to be pursued and valued. Pour out Your love through Your Spirit. Give her ears to hear Your voice telling her she is loved by You, her good Father. Help her to rest, seen and cherished in Your care tonight, Lord. Amen.

Lord, I know that I am loved by You because . . .

_____

_____

_____

_____

_____

And so we know and rely on the love God has for us. God is love. Whoever lives in love lives in God, and God in them.

1 John 4:16

night
160

Lord, I pray for the woman reading this right now who **is struggling to believe in You.** She has followed You for so long, but her heart has grown cold. Show Yourself to her and help her to see that running from You is not the answer. Draw near to her and help her to keep pressing on. Give her hunger for Your truth alone. Open her eyes to see You and renew her faith, Lord. Amen.

Lord, help my unbelief as I learn . . .

_____

_____

_____

_____

_____

Immediately the boy's father exclaimed, "I do believe; help me overcome my unbelief!"

Mark 9:24

night
161

Lord, I pray for the woman reading this right now who **wants to hunger for righteousness** (Matthew 5:6). Create in her a longing to know You more. Give her a deeper desire to meet You, to know You, and to live for You. Take her hunger for lesser things and replace it with a hunger to be satisfied in You alone. Help her to grow in wisdom as she follows You. Bless her in her obedience to You, Lord. Amen.

Lord, replace my hunger for . . .

_____

_____

_____

_____

_____

Blessed are those who hunger and thirst for righteousness, for they will be filled.

Matthew 5:6

night
162

Lord, I pray for the woman reading this right now who **has suffered for so long that she isn't sure she can take another step.** Be her strength and be her refuge, Lord. In this hard season, surround her and sustain her with who You are. Lift her and renew her spirit to have hope again. As she looks to You, restore the joy of her salvation (Psalm 51:12). Ease her pain as she clings to You tonight, Lord. Amen.

Lord, I need Your strength to continue . . .

_____

_____

_____

_____

_____

Restore to me the joy of your salvation and grant me a willing spirit, to sustain me.

Psalm 51:12

Lord, I pray for the woman reading this right now who **has been manipulated**. Don't let her carry the guilt that does not belong to her. Guard her heart against trying to replay what has happened. Comfort her, Lord. Allow her to trust again and bring healing and forgiveness. Give her wisdom to move forward, trusting You with each step. You are right there beside her, and You won't leave her. Cover her with Your grace and be near her tonight, Lord. Amen.

Lord, I will not let what happened make me . . .

_____

_____

_____

_____

Vindicate me, my God, and plead my cause against an unfaithful nation. Rescue me from those who are deceitful and wicked.

Psalm 43:1

night
164

Lord, I pray for the woman reading this right now who **is longing to be close to You.** Give her the desires of her heart. Come close to her and allow her to feel Your presence. Fill her with Your love. Help her to rest in just being loved and known and treasured by You. Lord, may she know the love of Christ that is beyond knowledge so that she will be filled with the fullness of God (Ephesians 3:19). Amen.

Lord, I will continue to draw close to You by . . .

_____

_____

_____

_____

_____

And to know this love that surpasses knowledge—that you may be filled to the measure of all the fullness of God.

Ephesians 3:19

Lord, I pray for the woman reading this right now who **is ready to give up.** Renew her strength and energy. Give her a new hunger for what You have called her to, Lord. Protect her from discouragement and believing that her work does not matter. She has purpose and significance. Help her to serve You from a willing and humble heart, and supply her with exactly what she needs to keep going, Lord. Amen.

Lord, give me the strength to keep . . .

_____

_____

_____

_____

_____

Save me, O God, by your name; vindicate me by your might.

Psalm 54:1

night
166

Lord, I pray for the woman reading this right now who **is struggling to let go of things from her past.** Give her grace to accept where she has been and to entrust those mistakes to You, Lord. You see her, and You love her just as she is. Don't let her be crippled by what she thinks is failure. Use the past to shape her future as she follows You. Remind her that You bring redemption and grace, and that You can use her story for Your glory, Lord. Amen.

Lord, I give You the past by . . .

_____

_____

_____

_____

Forgetting what is behind and straining toward what is ahead, I press on toward the goal to win the prize for which God has called me heavenward in Christ Jesus.

Philippians 3:13–14

Lord, I pray for the woman reading this right now who **wonders if anyone really cares**. She has been through so much, and she feels so alone. You know her pain, Jesus. As she longs for friendship, be a faithful companion to her. Help her meet You in her loneliness and discover that You are a friend to the brokenhearted. You are beside her all of her days and she can find consolation in You, Lord. Amen.

Lord, when I feel alone, I will . . .

_____

_____

_____

_____

_____

Turn to me and be gracious to me, for I am lonely and afflicted.

Psalm 25:16

Lord, I pray for the woman reading this right now who **is ready for a fresh outlook on life.** Create in her a new heart and renewed vision for what You want for her. Help her to stay close to You and guard her heart from chasing what she wants, Lord. The things of this world can threaten to steal her gaze from You, so lead her to do Your will in this season and to love You first. Cover her with Your grace as she follows You, Lord. Amen.

Lord, renew my heart for . . .

_____

_____

_____

_____

But I pray to you, Lord, in the time of your favor; in your great love, O God, answer me with your sure salvation.

Psalm 69:13

Lord, I pray for the woman reading this right now who **is tired of being lukewarm in her faith** (Revelation 3:15–16). She wants to give her whole life—every part of who she is—to You. She wants to trust You completely. Teach her to obey You each day in what is before her. Enable her to fulfill the mundane routines and tasks with great love for You and others. Help her to be patient with the growth and change she is experiencing. You see her love for You, and there is grace as she learns to follow You, Lord. Amen.

Lord, I need You to refresh and renew my faith by . . .

_____

_____

_____

I know your deeds, that you are neither cold nor hot. I wish you were either one or the other! So, because you are lukewarm—neither hot nor cold—I am about to spit you out of my mouth.

Revelation 3:15–16

Lord, I pray for the woman reading this right now who **needs Your defense and protection from the enemy.** She feels hopeless and helpless, Lord. Protect her heart from discouragement and despair. Give her the strength to turn toward You instead of away from You. Bring healing and the assurance that with You, a new day and a new season are always possible. She can trust You to come to her defense and cover her with Your wings (Psalm 91:3–4). Be so near to her tonight, Lord. Amen.

Lord, I will not lose hope for . . .

_____

_____

_____

Surely he will save you from the fowler's snare and from the deadly pestilence. He will cover you with his feathers, and under his wings you will find refuge; his faithfulness will be your shield and rampart.

Psalm 91:3–4

Lord, I pray for the woman reading this right now who **has lost someone she loves.** She is gripped by pain and fear, and even regret. Meet her in her sorrow, Lord. Open Your arms to her as she grieves all she thought would be. Embrace her with Your never-changing love. Bring healing, hope, and comfort to her heart. Show her the way forward from here. Be her strong tower as she finds safety and strength in You, Lord (Proverbs 18:10). Amen.

Lord, comfort my heart from the overwhelming loss of . . .

_____

_____

_____

_____

The name of the Lord is a fortified tower; the righteous run to it and are safe.

Proverbs 18:10

night
172

Lord, I pray for the woman reading this right now who **feels the fog of darkness around her will not lift**. Surround her with Your presence and Your peace tonight. Invade her life with the light of Your love and show her that how she feels does not come from You. Ease her mind and bring safety as she trusts that Your angels are guarding her (Psalm 91:11). Restore her hope and joy. Lift her eyes to You and give her the sacredness of Your presence, Lord. Amen.

Lord, as I step out of the dark and trust You in the light, I will . . .

_____

_____

_____

_____

For he will command his angels concerning you to guard you in all your ways.

Psalm 91:11

Lord, I pray for the woman reading this right now who **needs faith**. She knows she should believe You, but she is struggling. Pour out Your Spirit and renew her faith. Give her confidence and help her to trust in You. Overwhelm her with Your peace and help her believe in better days ahead. When she is wavering, help her to remember Your faithfulness in the past, Lord. Amen.

Lord, give me faith to believe . . .

_____

_____

_____

_____

_____

The apostles said to the Lord, "Increase our faith!"

Luke 17:5

night
174

Lord, I pray for the woman reading this right now who **feels her life is going nowhere fast.** Use these feelings of apathy to draw her closer to You and give her eyes to see where sin may be taking root. Renew her desires to serve You and glorify You with her life. Out of Your kindness, lead her through this season to refine her and purify her. Give her grace as she walks obediently with You no matter how she feels, Lord. Amen.

Lord, help me to see why I feel stuck in . . .

_____

_____

_____

Though the fig tree does not bud and there are no grapes on the vines, though the olive crop fails and the fields produce no food, though there are no sheep in the pen and no cattle in the stalls, yet I will rejoice in the Lord, *I will be joyful in God my Savior.*

Habakkuk 3:17–18

night
175

Lord, I pray for the woman reading this right now who **feels alone in her suffering.** Jesus, You know what she is walking through. Remind her that You suffer with her. You understand her and care for her. She is never alone. Draw close to her and ease her pain, Lord. Bring supernatural healing and hope to her circumstances. Help her to have faith that You are with her and You won't let her go, Lord. Amen.

Lord, in my suffering, I will make the choice to . . .

_____

_____

_____

_____

_____

Lord, do not forsake me; do not be far from me, my God. Come quickly to help me, my Lord and my Savior.

Psalm 38:21–22

night
176

Lord, I pray for the woman reading this right now who **needs wisdom and understanding to follow Your purposes for her**. She wants to follow You, but she isn't sure where You are leading. Show her what You are preparing her for, Lord. Open doors for her and go before her. Make the crooked paths straight (Isaiah 45:2) and use what she is enduring right now for Your plans. Help her to trust in Your will and Your way, Lord. Amen.

Lord, as I wait for what is next, use . . .

_____

_____

_____

_____

I will go before you and make the crooked places straight; I will break in pieces the gates of bronze and cut the bars of iron.

Isaiah 45:2 NKJV

night
177

Lord, I pray for the woman reading this right now who **is struggling with spiritual attacks from the enemy.** Surround her and guard her. Be a shield of protection for her. Remind her that she does not fight in her own strength but in the strength of the Lord (2 Thessalonians 3:3). Give her faith to declare and stand strong in Your victorious name, Jesus. Be near to her as she finds safety in You, Lord. Amen.

Lord, it is in Your name, Jesus,
that I declare the enemy must flee with his attacks of . . .

_____

_____

_____

_____

But the Lord is faithful, who will establish you and guard you from the evil one.

2 Thessalonians 3:3 NKJV

Lord, I pray for the woman reading this right now who **wishes her life looked different**. Open her eyes to what she has instead of what she wishes she had. Enable her to let go of expectations and envy. Give her the ability to accept her life, not as a mistake, but as what You are using to draw her closer to You. You have a perfect plan for her, and she can trust You. Help her to walk confidently in that truth tonight, Lord. Amen.

Lord, even though my life isn't what I expected, I accept . . .

_____

_____

_____

_____

Since, then, you have been raised with Christ, set your hearts on things above, where Christ is, seated at the right hand of God.

Colossians 3:1

Lord, I pray for the woman reading this right now who **isn't sure how to take the next step**. She is tired of all the hard stuff, and she is struggling to get through each day. Strengthen her, Lord. Give her peace and open her eyes to how You are working even in the pain. Help her to give over her circumstances to You and surrender the outcomes to You. She can trust Your perfect plan for her life. Soothe her in her suffering and wrap her in Your embrace tonight, Lord. Amen.

Lord, give me the strength today to . . .

_____

_____

_____

_____

Yes, Lord, walking in the way of your laws, we wait for you; your name and renown are the desire of our hearts.

Isaiah 26:8

night
180

Lord, I pray for the woman reading this right now who **wishes You didn't feel so far away**. Come close to her. Speak to her and renew her faith. Deepen her hope in You and give her a new sense of Your presence. Absolutely nothing can separate her from the love You have for her, Lord (Romans 8:38–39). You are there with her. Fill her with joy and peace that is beyond words and understanding tonight. Amen.

Lord, reveal Your presence in . . .

_____

_____

_____

_____

For I am convinced that neither death nor life, neither angels nor demons, neither the present nor the future, nor any powers, neither height nor depth, nor anything else in all creation, will be able to separate us from the love of God that is in Christ Jesus our Lord.

Romans 8:38–39

night
181

Lord, I pray for the woman reading this right now who **wants a pure heart**. Fill her, Holy Spirit, and create in her a clean heart (Psalm 51:10). Reveal areas in her life she needs to turn over to You. Help her to hunger and thirst for Your righteousness. Remind her of the pure heart You have given her through Jesus by Your death and resurrection. Cover her with Your grace as she humbly seeks You, Lord. Amen.

Lord, by Your grace,
help me to overcome sin and have a pure heart by . . .

_____

_____

_____

_____

_____

Create in me a pure heart, O God, and renew a steadfast spirit within me.

Psalm 51:10

night
182

Lord, I pray for the woman reading this right now who **wonders why bad things happen to good people.** She is questioning Your goodness and wondering if You even care. Reassure her that You are not "punishing her." Help her to see that You have already paid the price our sins require, Jesus. Increase her faith and faithfulness. Prevent her from growing discouraged and open her eyes to the ways You are working even through the hard stuff, Lord. Amen.

Lord, guard my heart against growing discouraged with . . .

_____

_____

_____

_____

For God did not send his Son into the world to condemn the world, but to save the world through him.

John 3:17

Lord, I pray for the woman reading this right now who **needs Your knowledge and help to make a decision she is wrestling with.** You have promised that You will give us wisdom when we ask for it. So give her insight and direction. Give her discernment to know what is from You and what is not. As she seeks You, protect her from any desire or thought that is not Your will. Help her to surrender this choice to You and to trust Your way is best, Lord. Amen.

Lord, give me the wisdom to know . . .

_____

_____

_____

_____

_____

Set your minds on things above, not on earthly things.

Colossians 3:2

Lord, I pray for the woman reading this right now who **is tired of her hard life**. Lighten her load and give her relief. In the midst of her hard circumstances, open her eyes to what others are going through as well. Increase her love and compassion for those around her. Pour out Your Spirit to renew her passion and love for You. Fix her eyes on You, Jesus, who, out of Your love for us, endured the cross (Hebrews 12:2). Amen.

Lord, when I feel tired and burdened, I will remind myself of . . .

_____

_____

_____

_____

Fixing our eyes on Jesus, the pioneer and perfecter of faith. For the joy set before him he endured the cross, scorning its shame, and sat down at the right hand of the throne of God.

Hebrews 12:2

Lord, I pray for the woman reading this right now who **desperately wants to break her cycle of unhealth.** She has been living by her own standards, with unhealthy habits, and she is weary of her ways. Convict her, but also comfort her. Bring repentance and bring restoration. You alone bring change and growth. So help her to turn to You in faith. Cover her with Your grace and be so near to her tonight, Lord. Amen.

Lord, in order to continue to heal, I know I need to turn from . . .

_____

_____

_____

_____

Do you not know that your bodies are temples of the Holy Spirit, who is in you, whom you have received from God? You are not your own; you were bought at a price. Therefore honor God with your bodies.

1 Corinthians 6:19–20

night
186

Lord, I pray for the woman reading this right now who **feels devastated by her situation**. Out of her poverty, bring hope. Take whatever feels shattered and piece it back together again, Lord. Remake her and restore her. Use whatever has broken her to make her whole again. You are the Healer and Restorer, and nothing is impossible for You (Luke 1:37). Help her to trust in You tonight, Lord. Amen.

Lord, I give You the pieces that have been broken by . . .

_____

_____

_____

_____

_____

For no word from God will ever fail.

Luke 1:37

Lord, I pray for the woman reading this right now who **is struggling to feel grateful for her life.** Help her to see all that You have given her, Lord. Root out the sin of envy and guard her heart against the temptation to compare or compete. Fill her with thanksgiving and increasing awareness of all You have done for her in the past and continue to do today. Give her eyes to see the good. May she humbly come before You in repentance and with praise tonight, Lord. Amen.

Lord, help me overcome my envy of . . .

_____

_____

_____

_____

Praise the Lord, my soul; all my inmost being, praise his holy name.
Praise the Lord, my soul, and forget not all his benefits.

Psalm 103:1–2

night
188

Lord, I pray for the woman reading this right now who **feels insecure in what You've called her to.** Cultivate in her courage. Grow faith and confidence in her. Remind her of the gifts You have given her and that it is Your work in and through her. Nothing she does is without You (John 15:5). You will give her the strength she needs to accomplish what You've called her to. Enable her to bear fruit as she continues to abide in You, Lord. Amen.

Lord, I will walk with confidence into . . .

_____

_____

_____

_____

*I am the vine; you are the branches. If you remain in me and I in you,
you will bear much fruit; apart from me you can do nothing.*

John 15:5

Lord, I pray for the woman reading this right now who **is devastated by the loss of a dream.** Allow her to grieve honestly with You. Be tender with her and show Your love for her, Lord. Give her Your perspective and help her to see that Your desires are greater than her dreams. She can trust You to show her a new way, a better way. Stay close to her as she surrenders her hopes to You, Lord. Amen.

Lord, to You, I surrender my dream of . . .

_____

_____

_____

_____

If I say, "Surely the darkness will hide me and the light become night around me," even the darkness will not be dark to you; the night will shine like the day, for darkness is as light to you.

Psalm 139:11–12

night
190

Lord, I pray for the woman reading this right now who **is ready for something different**. Give her patience as she waits on You. Prepare her for what is next in her life. Don't let her just rush through this season or these circumstances, but teach her and grow her as she waits for direction from You. When the time is right, lead her into something new with a heart that is willing to walk in Your way, wherever that is and whatever that may be, Lord. Amen.

Lord, in Your kindness, open a door to . . .

_____

_____

_____

_____

_____

But if we hope for what we do not yet have, we wait for it patiently.

Romans 8:25

night
191

Lord, I pray for the woman reading this right now who **wants to seek You with all her heart** (Psalm 119:10). She has a deep desire to know You and serve You. Fill her, Holy Spirit. Give her the grace to turn from old ways or habits. Set her free from any sin that may be entangling her. Empower her to run the race marked out for her (Hebrews 12:1) with joy and gratitude for all You've done. Give her grace as she follows You, Lord. Amen.

Lord, set me free from . . .

_____

_____

_____

_____

_____

I seek you with all my heart; do not let me stray from your commands.

Psalm 119:10

Lord, I pray for the woman reading this right now who **needs help**. Her life seems unmanageable, and she doesn't know where to turn. Don't let her heart turn away from You in the chaos, but help her to turn to You for everything she needs. Deliver her from all that is weighing her down and send Your Spirit to guide her and teach her (John 14:26). Be her refuge and salvation, Lord. Make a way for her and answer her cries for help. Amen.

Lord, I need Your help with . . .

_____

_____

_____

_____

But the Advocate, the Holy Spirit, whom the Father will send in my name, will teach you all things and will remind you of everything I have said to you.

John 14:26

night
193

Lord, I pray for the woman reading this right now who **needs joy**. Take away any discouragement she might be feeling. Pierce her darkness with Your overwhelming light. Lift the cloud that she feels is surrounding her. Pour out Your light and love in her heart. Renew her happiness in You and give her a genuine spirit of contentment as she finds peace in following You, Lord. Amen.

Lord, give me joy once again in . . .

_____

_____

_____

_____

_____

Let me hear joy and gladness; let the bones you have crushed rejoice.

Psalm 51:8

night
194

Lord, I pray for the woman reading this right now who **is anxious for tomorrow**. Don't let her be consumed with what the next day holds but protect her from fear and worry. Saturate and control her mind with peace. Remind her that You can be trusted with her future. Each day has enough worries of its own (Matthew 6:34). You are her Provider and Protector; and you will give her everything she needs. Help her to rest in peace tonight, Lord. Amen.

Lord, even though I don't know what tomorrow will bring, I trust You will . . .

_____

_____

_____

_____

Therefore do not worry about tomorrow, for tomorrow will worry about itself. Each day has enough trouble of its own.

Matthew 6:34

night
195

Lord, I pray for the woman reading this right now who **needs the courage to pick up the phone and ask for help.** She doesn't want to burden others and is afraid of what they will think. Give her the bravery to just ask. Send godly counsel her way. Surround her with the right kind of people and supply her with the help she needs through Your strength and the generosity of others. Be with her as she steps out in faith, Lord. Amen.

Lord, I will seek help by . . .

_____

_____

_____

_____

_____

Carry each other's burdens, and in this way you will fulfill the law of Christ.

Galatians 6:2

night
196

Lord, I pray for the woman reading this right now who **wants to surrender her life to You.** Give her the wisdom to take the next step of trusting You with her life. Whether that is big or small, show her where she can follow You more fully and faithfully. Honor her obedience to You. Show her the blessing that comes from walking closely with You (Psalm 1:1–3). Envelope her with Your love as she loves You, Lord. Amen.

Lord, as a next step of faithfulness, I will . . .

_____

_____

_____

_____

Blessed is the one who does not walk in step with the wicked or stand in the way that sinners take or sit in the company of mockers, but whose delight is in the law of the Lord, and who meditates on his law day and night.

Psalm 1:1–2

Lord, I pray for the woman reading this right now who **feels lost**. Make straight paths for her. No matter what she is walking through, give her the right feet—careful and steadfast (Proverbs 4:26). Steady her and direct her. Be close to her and show her she is not alone. You are right there beside her, and she can trust You. Help her to feel Your presence tonight, Lord. Amen.

Lord, deliver me from . . .

_____

_____

_____

_____

_____

Give careful thought to the paths for your feet and be steadfast in all your ways.

Proverbs 4:26

night
198

Lord, I pray for the woman reading this right now who **is struggling to control her emotions.** Invite her to come to You openly and honestly. Help her to control what she feels and enable her to honor You with her emotions. Open her eyes to the ways she has let her guard down and given in to the way she feels instead of to what the truth is. She can rest securely in Your unchanging Word and Your steadfast love for her, Lord. Amen.

Lord, give me victory by controlling the emotion of . . .

_____

_____

_____

_____

Better a patient person than a warrior, one with self-control than one who takes a city.

Proverbs 16:32

Lord, I pray for the woman reading this right now who **wishes she had a second chance.** Remind her of how deep and wide Your mercy is. Every day is an opportunity, by Your grace, to begin again. She doesn't have to live in the past because You are the God who redeems all things (Ephesians 1:7). Pour out Your love and Your kindness to her. Empower her to walk in the newness of life You offer, Lord. Amen.

Lord, I choose to believe Your mercy is enough to forgive me of . . .

_____

_____

_____

_____

_____

In him we have redemption through his blood, the forgiveness of sins, in accordance with the riches of God's grace.

Ephesians 1:7

night
200

Lord, I pray for the woman reading this right now who **is frustrated with her life**. Protect her heart from anger and discouragement. Soften her heart. Give her patience and perseverance. Help her to honor You even when things are not going the way she wanted or expected. Work in this season and use it to draw her closer to You, Lord. Amen.

Lord, when I am frustrated, I will remember that . . .

_____

_____

_____

_____

_____

_____

Fools give full vent to their rage, but the wise bring calm in the end.

Proverbs 29:11

night
201

Lord, I pray for the woman reading this right now who **longs for a community that cheers one another on.** Show her favor by giving her friends who will be an encouragement and a support to her. Give her the joy of knowing deep and meaningful relationships that aren't threatened when someone else succeeds. And help her to be patient, letting those friendships grow and mature at the right time and in the right way, Lord. Amen.

Lord, I will begin to cultivate friendship by . . .

_____

_____

_____

_____

Therefore encourage one another and build each other up, just as in fact you are doing.

1 Thessalonians 5:11

night
202

Lord, I pray for the woman reading this right now who **is struggling with an ungrateful heart**. Soften and create in her a new heart, one that is thankful for all that You have given her. Bring transformation and renewal that only Your Spirit can bring. Help her to see your good gifts all around her and the delight that can be found in them (1 Timothy 6:17). Give her a deep and lasting joy as she looks to You, Lord. Amen.

Lord, forgive me for being ungrateful with . . .

_____

_____

_____

_____

Command those who are rich in this present world not to be arrogant nor to put their hope in wealth, which is so uncertain, but to put their hope in God, who richly provides us with everything for our enjoyment.

1 Timothy 6:17

Lord, I pray for the woman reading this right now who **needs to know You see her**. You are with her and know every detail of her life. You care about and even promise to reward what is done in secret (Matthew 6:6). Give her an undivided heart to live for Your approval alone. Unite her will with Yours and help her to sense Your presence in every area of her life, Lord. Amen.

Lord, as I know You are looking upon me, I will faithfully continue to . . .

_____

_____

_____

_____

But when you pray, go into your room, close the door and pray to your Father, who is unseen. Then your Father, who sees what is done in secret, will reward you.

Matthew 6:6

night
204

Lord, I pray for the woman reading this right now who **needs You**. You have promised to be our strength when we are weak. She can trust You to come through for her. Give her Your grace. Be a rock and firm foundation for her. Remind her that You will not abandon her or leave her on her own (Joshua 1:5). Show her Your power, Your mercy, and Your love, Lord. Amen.

Lord, in my strength, I can't . . .

_____

_____

_____

_____

_____

No one will be able to stand against you all the days of your life. As I was with Moses, so I will be with you; I will never leave you nor forsake you.

Joshua 1:5

Lord, I pray for the woman reading this right now who **is grieving the life she dreamed of**. Allow her to release those dreams and give them to You. Enable her to accept the past and to surrender it to You, Lord. Raise up new longings and dreams within her. Give her hope for something different that You may have for her. Help her to walk confidently and securely in Your perfect will, Lord. Amen.

Lord, I release my dream of . . .

_____

_____

_____

_____

_____

The grass withers and the flowers fall, but the word of our God endures forever.

Isaiah 40:8

night
206

Lord, I pray for the woman reading this right now who **is struggling with envy**. Turn her gaze to You and Your goodness. Help her to focus on all that You *have* given her and fill her with gratefulness, Lord. Capture her heart with Your generosity in her life. Give her eyes to see the needs of others and a heart that longs to serve and give, Lord. Amen.

Lord, I praise You for giving me . . .

_____

_____

_____

_____

_____

Let us not become conceited, provoking and envying each other.

Galatians 5:26

Lord, I pray for the woman reading this right now who **is open to hearing from You**. She wants to desire what You desire for her life. Speak to her, Holy Spirit, and surround her with friends or family members who can speak the truth to her in this season. Guard her desires and thoughts and align what she wants with Your will. Lead her and guide her in this season, Lord. Amen.

Lord, I am open to hearing what You are speaking to me about . . .

_____

_____

_____

_____

My son, pay attention to what I say; turn your ear to my words. Do not let them out of your sight, keep them within your heart; for they are life to those who find them and health to one's whole body.

Proverbs 4:20–22

night
208

Lord, I pray for the woman reading this right now who **wishes she knew what to do with her life.** Show her what You want for her. She feels aimless and uncertain. Don't let her walk in confusion, Lord. Guide her steps and open doors for her. Help her to see what You want and where You are leading her. She can trust Your leading, Lord. Amen.

Lord, show me what I should do as I follow You in . . .

_____

_____

_____

_____

_____

I cry out to God Most High, to God who fulfills his purpose for me.

Psalm 57:2 ESV

night
209

Lord, I pray for the woman reading this right now who **is frustrated with her friends**. Help her build space for those not-so-perfect friendships. Allow her to have grace and patience. Bring peace and agreement where there is tension. Enlarge her love for those friendships that are hard right now and help her to move toward them, not away from them. Cover this area of her life with Your grace, Lord. Amen.

Lord, what I need most in my friendships right now is . . .

_____

_____

_____

_____

_____

How good and pleasant it is when God's people live together in unity!

Psalm 133:1

night
210

Lord, I pray for the woman reading this right now who **feels she is falling apart.** Comfort her in this difficult time. Don't let her become overwhelmed. Give her perspective and help her to see that not all is lost. She can walk with hope and resilience in the face of adversity. Bring beauty out of her pain and joy to her hurting heart tonight, Lord. Amen.

Lord, be near me as I struggle with . . .

_____

_____

_____

_____

_____

Save me, O God, by your name; vindicate me by your might. Hear my prayer, O God; listen to the words of my mouth.

Psalm 54:1–2

Lord, I pray for the woman reading this right now who **is frustrated at home**. Even when she feels like she can't keep it all together, You have it under control. You will work out the details. Give her the strength and help she craves. Take care of all the details that she feels are falling through the cracks. Bring peace over her heart and her home. May it be a place of rest and refreshment, Lord. Amen.

Lord, change my heart and give me an attitude of . . .

_____

_____

_____

_____

_____

Say to him: "Long life to you! Good health to you and your household! And good health to all that is yours!"

1 Samuel 25:6

night
212

Lord, I pray for the woman reading this right now who **is struggling to hold on**. Hold her, Lord. Steady her and fill her with Your strong love. Reassure her that she is going to be okay. Nothing has taken You by surprise, and You are right by her side. Strengthen her with Your faithfulness and allow her to carry on, even when it feels impossible. Be so near to her tonight, Lord. Amen.

Lord, I need You to carry . . .

_____

_____

_____

_____

_____

You hem me in behind and before, and you lay your hand upon me.

Psalm 139:5

Lord, I pray for the woman reading this right now who **is feeling drained**. Refresh her and renew her. When she feels weak, supply her with the energy she needs. Fill her up emotionally, physically, and spiritually, Lord. Uphold her with Your strength and refresh her with Your peace. Give her the rest she so deeply desires tonight, Lord. Amen.

Lord, I need You to fill up my . . .

_____

_____

_____

_____

There remains, then, a Sabbath-rest for the people of God; for anyone who enters God's rest also rests from their works, just as God did from his. Let us, therefore, make every effort to enter that rest, so that no one will perish by following their example of disobedience.

Hebrews 4:9–11

night
214

Lord, I pray for the woman reading this right now who **is tired of always putting others' needs before her own.** Help her to create space to have time for herself and to meet with You. Help her understand that it is okay, even necessary, to care for her soul, Lord. Give her the freedom to do so. Allow her the opportunities she needs to care for herself so she can love more deeply and freely those around her. Restore her and renew her as she learns to find rest in You, Lord. Amen.

Lord, in order to better care for myself, I will . . .

_____

_____

_____

_____

You are my hiding place; you will protect me from trouble and surround me with songs of deliverance.

Psalm 32:7

Lord, I pray for the woman reading this right now who **is worried and wondering about what awaits her in the morning.** Calm her nerves, Lord. Assure her that You are in control and will supply exactly what she needs. Give her rest, as You are the One who never sleeps. She can trust that You will be watching over her as she sleeps (Psalm 4:8). Help her to hold on to You. Cover her with an unexplainable peace and settle her heart tonight, Lord. Amen.

Lord, I surrender my worries of . . .

_____

_____

_____

_____

In peace I will lie down and sleep, for you alone, Lord, make me dwell in safety.

Psalm 4:8

Lord, I pray for the woman reading this right now who **feels crushed by what she's been through.** She never imagined her life would look like this. Slowly and surely begin to heal her, Lord. You are not done with her. You have a new season for her. Take her hurt and pain and use it for Your glory. This time has not been wasted, and she can trust You to bring hope out of her hurt. Be so near to her tonight, Lord. Amen.

Lord, in time, I am trusting You will use the pain of . . .

_____

_____

_____

_____

_____

Lord my God, I called to you for help, and you healed me.

Psalm 30:2

Lord, I pray for the woman reading this right now who **wants to follow You.** She has wrestled for so long, and she is ready to surrender to You. Invite her to come closer and just take the next step of obedience. Help her to let go of anything she might be holding on to from her past. She can trust You for what lies ahead. Give her confidence that her future with You is filled with peace and hope, Lord. Amen.

Lord, to follow You, I know I need to let go of . . .

_____

_____

_____

_____

Walk in obedience to all that the LORD your God has commanded you, so that you may live and prosper and prolong your days in the land that you will possess.

Deuteronomy 5:33

night
218

Lord, I pray for the woman reading this right now who **needs Your healing**. Restore her and give her what she needs to put the pieces of her life back together. Make her whole again, Lord. You have so much more for her. Keep her from minimizing her pain, but also don't let her be consumed by it. Give her Your peace as she finds hope in You, Lord.

Lord, come and heal my . . .

_____

_____

_____

_____

_____

Have mercy on me, LORD, for I am faint; heal me, LORD, for my bones are in agony.

Psalm 6:2

Lord, I pray for the woman reading this right now who **is struggling to keep going.** Don't let her mind drift into the worries of tomorrow. Just give her what she needs for today. Give her strength to keep taking the next step and the next step and the next step. Pour out Your Spirit and sustain her in her weakness. Though she feels weak, You are strong (2 Corinthians 12:10). She can trust Your care for her tonight, Lord. Amen.

Lord, I need a fresh outpouring of Your Spirit to strengthen my . . .

_____

_____

_____

_____

That is why, for Christ's sake, I delight in weaknesses, in insults, in hardships, in persecutions, in difficulties. For when I am weak, then I am strong.

2 Corinthians 12:10

night
220

Lord, I pray for the woman reading this right now who **is scared she'll mess up again.** Reassure her that perfection does not belong to her; it belongs to You. It is who You are, not who we are, that settles our soul and gives us peace, Lord. In Your love, continue to draw her to You, deepen her faith, and increase her faithfulness. You are a kind and gentle Father, and she can trust You tonight, Lord. Amen.

Lord, change my motivation to love You by . . .

_____

_____

_____

_____

_____

For all have sinned and fall short of the glory of God, and all are justified freely by his grace through the redemption that came by Christ Jesus.

Romans 3:23–24

Lord, I pray for the woman reading this right now who **needs a break**. She is struggling, feeling tired mentally and physically. Remind her that You are her rest, Lord. Surround her with Your presence and Your peace. Take her weary heart and breathe new life into it. Refresh her and renew her as she finds strength in You. Cover her with Your care and be near her tonight, Lord. Amen.

Lord, I will find rest by taking the step of . . .

_____

_____

_____

_____

_____

Look to the Lord and his strength; seek his face always.

1 Chronicles 16:11

night
222

Lord, I pray for the woman reading this right now who **wishes You would right all the wrongs that have been done to her.** Remind her of Your justice. You are the God who will set all things right one day. Help her to leave judgment and justice to You, Lord. Pour out Your love and give her patience and wisdom as she trusts Your way. Comfort her heart as she trusts that You will take care of her, Lord. Amen.

Lord, instead of trying to right the wrong, I will . . .

_____

_____

_____

_____

_____

Who will bring any charge against those whom God has chosen? It is God who justifies.

Romans 8:33

Lord, I pray for the woman reading this right now who **wonders why her life turned out like this.** She has followed You and been faithful to You, and she doesn't understand how You could let this happen to her. Help her to see that You work all things out for her good and for Your glory (Romans 8:28). Give her faith to see that what You have allowed You are using and You will continue to use. Comfort her heart tonight, Lord. Amen.

Lord, with faith, hope, and love I will accept . . .

_____

_____

_____

_____

And we know that in all things God works for the good of those who love him, who have been called according to his purpose.

Romans 8:28

night
224

Lord, I pray for the woman reading this right now who **wants to cultivate faithfulness and endurance within herself**. Deepen her relationship with You as she seeks Your heart. Build faith and hope in something stronger than her feelings about life's circumstances. Purify her faith and give her a deep love for Your Word. Speak to her and fill her as You work in her heart and life during this new season, Lord. Amen.

Lord, in this season, I need You to grow in me . . .

_____

_____

_____

_____

For everything that was written in the past was written to teach us, so that through the endurance taught in the Scriptures and the encouragement they provide we might have hope.

Romans 15:4

Lord, I pray for the woman reading this right now who **wants to see the good in the middle of what is so hard.** Open her eyes to see You and Your goodness. Give her faith to see not only what You will do but what You are doing. Help her to have the endurance and grit to stay strong no matter what each day holds. Fill her with faith and hope as she stays close to You, Lord. Amen.

Lord, even though this season is hard, I thank You for . . .

_____

_____

_____

_____

Finally, brothers and sisters, whatever is true, whatever is noble, whatever is right, whatever is pure, whatever is lovely, whatever is admirable—if anything is excellent or praiseworthy—think about such things.

Philippians 4:8

night
226

Lord, I pray for the woman reading this right now who **is bored with her life**. Renew her vibrancy for life and for following You. Help her to see that joy is not found in the "next thing." True joy and lasting satisfaction are found in knowing You, Lord (Psalm 16:11). There is no more exciting place than right in Your will. Draw close to her and refresh her love for You and Your Kingdom, Lord. Amen.

Lord, what I need most right now is to return to . . .

_____

_____

_____

_____

_____

You make known to me the path of life; you will fill me with joy in your presence, with eternal pleasures at your right hand.

Psalm 16:11

Lord, I pray for the woman reading this right now who **wonders what You have for her.** Would you show her Your kindness and reveal to her what is to come? Help her to wait patiently, Lord. Grow humility and dependence within her as she looks to You. In her wondering, align her heart with Yours. May she not turn to the left or to the right, but help her to surrender to Your perfect plan tonight, Lord. Amen.

Lord, as I wait on You, give me a heart that . . .

_____

_____

_____

_____

Many are the plans in a person's heart, but it is the Lord's purpose that prevails.

Proverbs 19:21

night
228

Lord, I pray for the woman reading this right now who **is unmoved by her sin**. In Your kindness, lead her to repentance. Convict her and soften her heart, Lord. Open her eyes to the deceptiveness of sin and help her to see that what You are offering her is better than anything this world has to offer. Cover her with Your grace and forgiveness as she turns to You tonight, Lord. Amen.

Lord, soften my heart as I confess my sin of . . .

_____

_____

_____

_____

_____

If we claim to be without sin, we deceive ourselves and the truth is not in us.

1 John 1:8

Lord, I pray for the woman reading this right now who **wonders why You aren't listening to her prayers**. Remind her that prayer is meant to change her heart instead of Yours. Teach her that You do hear her, and You love her (Psalm 34:17). You are working in ways that perhaps she cannot see or understand right now. Be near to her tonight, Lord. Amen.

Lord, answer my prayers for . . .

_____

_____

_____

_____

_____

The righteous cry out, and the LORD hears them; he delivers them from all their troubles.

Psalm 34:17

night
230

Lord, I pray for the woman reading this right now who **feels detached from everything and everyone.** Give her an understanding of why she feels this way. Help her to see the need for engagement. Protect her from slowly drifting and instead draw her closer to You. Soften her heart and renew her love for You and for others. Bring her joy as she learns to walk in fellowship with friends again, Lord. Amen.

Lord, I will move toward others by taking the step of . . .

_____

_____

_____

_____

_____

Yet I am always with you; you hold me by my right hand.

Psalm 73:23

Lord, I pray for the woman reading this right now who **is hurting because of the words someone spoke over her.** Silence any lies she is hearing. Drown out the voices from her past. Give her ears to hear Your voice alone. Holy Spirit, speak loudly and clearly to her. As she lies down to sleep tonight, remind her that she is loved and cherished by You (Isaiah 54:10). Hold her close, Lord. Amen.

Lord, help me to remember what You say about me when I . . .

_____

_____

_____

_____

"Though the mountains be shaken and the hills be removed, yet my unfailing love for you will not be shaken nor my covenant of peace be removed," says the Lord, who has compassion on you.

Isaiah 54:10

night
232

Lord, I pray for the woman reading this right now who **wonders what this next season will be like.** She is anxious about what is to come and is hoping for good things. Bless her, Lord. Show her Your favor and faithfulness. Be kind and gracious to her. And show her she doesn't need to worry. She is safe with You and she can rest in that truth tonight, Lord. Amen.

Lord, take away my fear of . . .

_____

_____

_____

_____

_____

There is a time for everything, and a season for every activity under the heavens.

Ecclesiastes 3:1

Lord, I pray for the woman reading this right now who **is ready to turn her life around**. Give her wisdom and the power to take the next step of letting go of her past. Show her where she needs to move forward in obedience in following You. Protect her as she gives You her future. Pour out Your mercy and grace in her life as she walks faithfully with You, Lord. Amen.

Lord, I will begin to turn my life over to You by . . .

_____

_____

_____

_____

_____

I will give them an undivided heart and put a new spirit in them; I will remove from them their heart of stone and give them a heart of flesh.

Ezekiel 11:19

night
234

Lord, I pray for the woman reading this right now who **wonders if You are real.** Help her unbelief. Show Yourself to her, Lord. Increase her faith and hope. Remind her that times of doubt can lead to greater devotion and ultimately greater peace. Give her wisdom and answer the cry of her heart to see You, know You, and experience Your loving presence tonight, Lord. Amen.

*Lord, You have promised to never leave me,
and so I will show my trust by . . .*

_____

_____

_____

_____

Then you will call on me and come and pray to me, and I will listen to you. You will seek me and find me when you seek me with all your heart.
Jeremiah 29:12–13

Lord, I pray for the woman reading this right now who **has hurt others with her words**. Forgive her and allow her to see why she said what she said. Soften her heart, Lord. Give her the courage to make it right and to seek peace with those she has hurt and offended. Turn her words into instruments of life, not death (Romans 6:13), and help her to love others well with her words, Lord. Amen.

Lord, forgive me for using my words against . . .

_____

_____

_____

_____

Do not offer any part of yourself to sin as an instrument of wickedness, but rather offer yourselves to God as those who have been brought from death to life; and offer every part of yourself to him as an instrument of righteousness.

Romans 6:13

night
236

Lord, I pray for the woman reading this right now who **has been going full speed for so long that she isn't sure how to slow down.** Settle her heart, Lord. Show her where she needs to pull back or the things she needs to give up and let go of. Help her to pursue what is most important in this season of her life. Give her wisdom to know how to rest and help her to start by resting tonight, Lord. Amen.

Lord, one way I can begin to slow down is by . . .

_____

_____

_____

_____

_____

The plans of the diligent lead to profit as surely as haste leads to poverty.

Proverbs 21:5

Lord, I pray for the woman reading this right now who **is seeking Your truth.** Speak to her through Your Word. Open her ears and open her eyes to what You want to say to her and what You want to teach her. Protect her from being led astray and guide her, Holy Spirit, by leading her to greater faithfulness to Jesus, who is the way, the truth, and the life (John 14:6). Fill her with Your wisdom as she seeks You, Lord. Amen.

Lord, I will seek Your truth by . . .

_____

_____

_____

_____

Jesus answered, "I am the way and the truth and the life. No one comes to the Father except through me."

John 14:6

Lord, I pray for the woman reading this right now who **is tired of making the same mistakes over and over again.** Protect her from growing discouraged and from giving up. Empower her to begin again, Lord. Guard her mind against focusing on the past (Isaiah 43:18). Don't let her be consumed with her mistakes. Encounter her with Your mercy and allow her to experience Your unconditional love tonight, Lord. Amen.

Lord, give me Your grace to overcome . . .

_____

_____

_____

_____

Forget the former things; do not dwell on the past.

Isaiah 43:18

Lord, I pray for the woman reading this right now who **can't find her way out of the hopelessness she feels**. Protect her and be her strong Deliverer in this battle (Psalm 140:7). Make a way for her in this desert time, Lord. Come to her rescue and be her salvation. You are the God of hope and freedom and joy. She can lean wholly on You no matter what she is going through. Be with her tonight, Lord. Amen.

Lord, I need hope to . . .

_____

_____

_____

_____

_____

Sovereign Lord, my strong deliverer, you shield my head in the day of battle.

Psalm 140:7

Lord, I pray for the woman reading this right now who **wonders if she's making a difference.** Consume her and concern her more with Your love first. As she walks in faithfulness, she can trust You to use her. Free her heart and mind from worrying about fruit or fruitfulness. You supply the seed and increase the harvest (2 Corinthians 9:10). Give her confidence that You are working whether she sees it or not, Lord. Amen.

Lord, free me from worrying about . . .

_____

_____

_____

_____

Now he who supplies seed to the sower and bread for food will also supply and increase your store of seed and will enlarge the harvest of your righteousness.

2 Corinthians 9:10

Lord, I pray for the woman reading this right now who **is struggling after loss**. Be a safe and secure place for her to weep and mourn what she thought her future would look like and who she would spend it with. Enable her to move forward with the hurt, and bring healing and hope in the midst of her loss. Hear the honest cries of her heart and bring consolation to her tonight, Lord. Amen.

Lord, as I grieve, I need healing to . . .

_____

_____

_____

_____

_____

"He will wipe every tear from their eyes. There will be no more death" or mourning or crying or pain, for the old order of things has passed away.

Revelation 21:4

night
242

Lord, I pray for the woman reading this right now who **is wrestling with past hurts.** Don't let her dwell on what has been. Just as You can be trusted with the future, You can be trusted with the past. Help her to release the hurts and entrust them into Your loving care. Let all bitterness and unforgiveness be removed and replace them with forgiveness (Ephesians 4:31–32). Give her a heart of acceptance and trust in Your good and loving plan, Lord. Amen.

Lord, I will trust You with my past by . . .

_____

_____

_____

_____

Get rid of all bitterness, rage and anger, brawling and slander, along with every form of malice. Be kind and compassionate to one another, forgiving each other, just as in Christ God forgave you.

Ephesians 4:31–32

Lord, I pray for the woman reading this right now who **wants to love her life but doesn't**. Help her to see how she can love and serve You right where she is. Give her an attitude of Christlike service to You. Change her focus from her circumstances and continue to draw her outward toward giving her life to others. Refresh her heart and give her renewed hope as she finds joy in You, Lord. Amen.

Lord, help me to keep my focus on . . .

_____

_____

_____

_____

_____

Now that I, your Lord and Teacher, have washed your feet, you also should wash one another's feet.

John 13:14

night
244

Lord, I pray for the woman reading this right now who **wonders why You feel so distant.** Show her that faith is deeper than how we feel. Give her a stronger faith, one that is anchored in trust and faithfulness, Lord. Open her heart to experience Your presence again. Bless her, console her, and show her that You are not really distant. You are in her midst (Zephaniah 3:17) tonight, Lord. Amen.

Lord, You feel far away but I know that You are close because . . .

_____

_____

_____

_____

The LORD your God is with you, the Mighty Warrior who saves. He will take great delight in you; in his love he will no longer rebuke you, but will rejoice over you with singing.

Zephaniah 3:17

Lord, I pray for the woman reading this right now who **wants to make the most of the time she has.** Carve out space for her to hear Your voice and give her wisdom to make the most of every opportunity because the days are evil (Ephesians 5:15–16). Help her know what to say yes to and what to say no to so she can make her days count. Overwhelm her with Your presence as she follows You in faithfulness, Lord. Amen.

Lord, I will guard my time by . . .

_____

_____

_____

_____

Be very careful, then, how you live—not as unwise but as wise, making the most of every opportunity, because the days are evil.

Ephesians 5:15–16

night
246

Lord, I pray for the woman reading this right now who **is longing for a deeper walk with You.** She has struggled to follow You with her whole heart, and she knows she needs to surrender her life to You. Reveal to her where she needs to take the next step of obedience. Show her the areas of her life where she can follow You more faithfully and more fully. Satisfy her longing to know You more, Lord. Amen.

Lord, I will draw closer to You by . . .

_____

_____

_____

_____

_____

Now faith is confidence in what we hope for and assurance about what we do not see.

Hebrews 11:1

Lord, I pray for the woman reading this right now who **needs You to dig her out of the hole she is in.** Deliver her from her hard circumstances. Show her Your love and comfort her with Your care as she lays down the things that have gotten her into this situation. Set her free and put her feet on solid ground with a firm place to stand (Psalm 40:1–2). Lead her forward into a new season and be her guide, Lord. Amen.

Lord, deliver me from . . .

_____

_____

_____

_____

I waited patiently for the Lord; he turned to me and heard my cry. He lifted me out of the slimy pit, out of the mud and mire; he set my feet on a rock and gave me a firm place to stand.

Psalm 40:1–2

night
248

Lord, I pray for the woman reading this right now who **wants to hope for good things but is afraid to.** Reveal Your heart to her. Expose any wrong ideas about who You are, Lord. You are a good Father, and You want good things for her. Give her faith to see that Your desire is to bless her and to show her Your kindness. You want life for her. It's okay to ask for and expect good from You. Assure her with Your love tonight, Lord. Amen.

Lord, I am believing and asking You to . . .

_____

_____

_____

_____

There is one body and one Spirit, just as you were called to one hope when you were called; one Lord, one faith, one baptism; one God and Father of all, who is over all and through all and in all.

Ephesians 4:4–6

Lord, I pray for the woman reading this right now who **feels no one understands her**. Draw her closer to You and show her that You know her better than anyone (Psalm 139:1–4). You understand her, Lord. Give her the grace to relate her pain to Yours. You hear her, are with her, and You love her. Show her that the more she is honest with You, the more intimate her relationship with You will be, Lord. Amen.

Lord, I bring my . . .

_____

_____

_____

_____

You have searched me, Lord, and you know me. You know when I sit and when I rise; you perceive my thoughts from afar. You discern my going out and my lying down; you are familiar with all my ways. Before a word is on my tongue you, Lord, know it completely.

Psalm 139:1–4

night
250

Lord, I pray for the woman reading this right now who **has been struggling with a hard decision for what feels like forever**. Bring clarity where it is lacking and give her insight where she feels confused, Lord. Lead her and reveal to her what You want her to do. Help her to trust You with where You are guiding her and make a straight path for her, Lord. Amen.

Lord, give me wisdom with . . .

_____

_____

_____

_____

_____

For God is not a God of confusion but of peace.

1 Corinthians 14:33 ESV

Lord, I pray for the woman reading this right now who **needs You by her side**. She is struggling, and she feels like she can't take one more step. Meet her in her weakness. Sustain her by Your Spirit. Lift her eyes to You, Jesus, the author and perfecter of our faith (Hebrews 12:2). Carry her when she feels like she can't carry on. Cover her with Your grace and give her joy where there is sadness, Lord. Amen.

Lord, I need You to carry the heavy burden of . . .

_____

_____

_____

_____

Fixing our eyes on Jesus, the pioneer and perfecter of faith. For the joy set before him he endured the cross, scorning its shame, and sat down at the right hand of the throne of God.

Hebrews 12:2

Lord, I pray for the woman reading this right now who **is struggling with bitterness.** Bring freedom and peace from her unsettling emotions. Root out any unrighteous and unresolved anger she feels. Help her to trust You and look to You to make right any way in which she feels she has been wronged. Give her a heart that wants to honor You with all of who she is and walk in the freedom of forgiveness, Lord. Amen.

Lord, as I surrender my bitterness, help me to . . .

_____

_____

_____

_____

See to it that no one falls short of the grace of God and that no bitter root grows up to cause trouble and defile many.

Hebrews 12:15

Lord, I pray for the woman reading this right now who **is afraid of wasting her life.** Don't let her be in a rush. Allow her to slow down and see what You are doing in her heart and in her life, Lord. Give her eyes to see the value and purpose of where You have her right now and why. In her waiting, help her to realize there is no time wasted by You (Ephesians 1:11). She can trust You to use her for Your glory, Lord. Amen.

Lord, if there is one thing I believe You are doing right now, it is . . .

_____

_____

_____

_____

In him we were also chosen, having been predestined according to the plan of him who works out everything in conformity with the purpose of his will.

Ephesians 1:11

Lord, I pray for the woman reading this right now who **feels she is wandering**. Direct her steps. Open her eyes to where You are working in her life, Lord. Go before her and give her wisdom to walk after You. Purify her desires and align her will with Yours. Cover her with Your grace and give her a renewed sense of Your purpose and direction tonight, Lord. Amen.

Lord, give me direction in the area of my . . .

_____

_____

_____

_____

The LORD will guide you always; he will satisfy your needs in a sun-scorched land and will strengthen your frame. You will be like a well-watered garden, like a spring whose waters never fail.

Isaiah 58:11

Lord, I pray for the woman reading this right now who **is struggling to keep up**. Overwhelm her with Your love and the truth that You are the One doing the work in and through her. Give her a greater dependence on You. And help her to see that You are faithful and that You will take care of all that she feels is falling through the cracks. Give her grace as she does the best she can, Lord. Amen.

Lord, be faithful in what feels like failure to . . .

But those who hope in the Lord will renew their strength.

Isaiah 40:31

night
256

Lord, I pray for the woman reading this right now who **wonders if her life will ever change**. Day after day, she prays and hopes and dreams, but it seems like it doesn't make a difference. Don't let her give up. Fill her with hope and hear her prayers for a new season. Make a way for her, Lord. She can walk in Your light, and she will not walk in darkness (John 12:46). Brighten her path ahead, Lord. Amen.

Lord, I will not give up as I wait for You to . . .

_____

_____

_____

_____

I have come into the world as a light, so that no one who believes in me should stay in darkness.

John 12:46

night
257

Lord, I pray for the woman reading this right now who **is wrestling with her past.** Help her to release what she has done. Give her the grace to let go of who she was, Lord. She is a new creation in You (2 Corinthians 5:17). Enable her to entrust the past into Your care and hope for a bright future. Guard her heart from being consumed with what she cannot control and instead help her to walk forward in the freedom You offer, Lord. Amen.

Lord, help me to walk forward as a new creation by . . .

_____

_____

_____

_____

Therefore, if anyone is in Christ, the new creation has come: The old has gone, the new is here!

2 Corinthians 5:17

night
258

Lord, I pray for the woman reading this right now who **wishes she could take a hiatus from all the things.** She is overwhelmed by life and needs Your peace. Teach her that rest is found in You alone (Psalm 62:1). Refresh her with Your presence. Make her burden light by surrounding her with Your love. Carry what feels unbearable to her right now, Lord. Amen.

Lord, it is too much to carry, and so I give You . . .

_____

_____

_____

_____

_____

Truly my soul finds rest in God; my salvation comes from him.

Psalm 62:1

Lord, I pray for the woman reading this right now who **is struggling with spiritual warfare**. Defend her and deliver her. Come to her rescue, Lord. Help her to stand strong in Your power. Be a shield around her and remind her that You have already won her victory (1 Corinthians 15:57). She can walk confidently in Your protection and rest comfortably in Your care tonight, Lord. Amen.

Lord, in Your Name, deliver me from . . .

_____

_____

_____

_____

_____

But thanks be to God! He gives us the victory through our Lord Jesus Christ.

1 Corinthians 15:57

night
260

Lord, I pray for the woman reading this right now who **is wrestling with doubt**. She doesn't have to pretend or be ashamed of the questions swirling around in her mind. She can bring them openly and honestly to You, Lord. Show her that doubt can lead to greater devotion. Help her to understand that she won't ever have all the answers, and that is okay. More than all the right answers, give her a greater trust, wonder, and awe of who You are, Lord. Amen.

Lord, even if I don't always understand, I will trust You by . . .

_____

_____

_____

_____

"Everything is possible for one who believes." Immediately the boy's father exclaimed, "I do believe; help me overcome my unbelief!"

Mark 9:23–24

Lord, I pray for the woman reading this right now who **feels burned-out**. Help her to see that it is okay to protect her time and have boundaries. Show her where she needs to disengage to be refueled and rooted in Your love. Remind her that her first priority is You and those closest to her that You've entrusted to her care. She can be confident that You will take care of what she can't. Open her heart to receive the real rest You want to give her tonight, Lord. Amen.

Lord, I will focus on You and protect my time by . . .

_____

_____

_____

_____

I am the vine; you are the branches. If you remain in me and I in you, you will bear much fruit; apart from me you can do nothing.

John 15:5

night
262

Lord, I pray for the woman reading this right now who **wants to believe in You but is struggling to see Your goodness in her life.** Guard her heart against the lie that her lack of comfort says something about Your character. You have a deeper purpose for her. Help her to see that even trials and suffering can be for our good as we draw closer to You. Give her a glimpse of Your grace tonight, Lord. Amen.

Lord, I know You are good because . . .

_____

_____

_____

_____

_____

The Lord is good to all; he has compassion on all he has made.

Psalm 145:9

Lord, I pray for the woman reading this right now who **needs Your direction**. Holy Spirit, guide her in truth (John 16:13). Enable her to give You control as she desires to make decisions with her life that honor and glorify You. Guard her heart against anything that is not of You or is not the best You have for her. Help her to be patient as she trusts in You to lead her tonight, Lord. Amen.

Lord, help me to know what to do with . . .

_____

_____

_____

_____

But when he, the Spirit of truth, comes, he will guide you into all the truth. He will not speak on his own; he will speak only what he hears, and he will tell you what is yet to come.

John 16:13

night
264

Lord, I pray for the woman reading this right now who **cares too much about what others think.** Deliver her from the approval of people and the need to be valued by anyone other than You. Set her free and saturate her with Your love and approval. Remind her of the beautiful treasure she is in Christ. She can rest tonight in Your unconditional love for her, Lord (1 John 4:9–10). Amen.

Lord, deliver me from seeking the approval of others in my . . .

_____

_____

_____

_____

This is how God showed his love among us: He sent his one and only Son into the world that we might live through him. This is love: not that we loved God, but that he loved us and sent his Son as an atoning sacrifice for our sins.

1 John 4:9–10

Lord, I pray for the woman reading this right now who **feels You are far away**. Give her faith to know that You are deepening her faith. You are taking her beyond feelings, inviting her to walk by faith and take You at Your Word. So help her not to give up or to give in to doubt. Soften her heart to keep seeking You. There is nowhere she can go that You aren't there with her (Psalm 139:7–10). Be so near to her tonight, Lord. Amen.

Lord, even when I don't feel Your presence, I will . . .

_____

_____

_____

Where can I go from your Spirit? Where can I flee from your presence?
If I go up to the heavens, you are there; if I make my bed in the depths,
you are there. If . . . I settle on the far side of the sea, even there your
hand will guide me, your right hand will hold me fast.

Psalm 139:7–10

night
266

Lord, I pray for the woman reading this right now who **is wrestling with an unhealthy relationship.** Give her wisdom about where she needs to set new boundaries. If necessary, give her the courage to distance herself from this person. Surround her with Your courage and peace, Lord. Comfort her heart as she makes hard decisions. Help her to trust that You will provide for her the right kind of relationships moving forward, Lord. Amen.

Lord, give me wisdom in my relationships by . . .

_____

_____

_____

_____

Walk with the wise and become wise, for a companion of fools suffers harm.

Proverbs 13:20

Lord, I pray for the woman reading this right now who **can't find her way**. Jesus, You are the way and the truth and the life (John 14:6). As she follows You, she is never truly wandering or lost. Lead her, like a good shepherd. Fill her with confidence that even when she feels disoriented, You are lovingly leading her. Show her Your grace and be near to her tonight, Lord. Amen.

Lord, even though I feel lost, I know You are leading me through . . .

_____

_____

_____

_____

_____

Jesus answered, "I am the way and the truth and the life. No one comes to the Father except through me."

John 14:6

Lord, I pray for the woman reading this right now who **is struggling to find peace.** Show her why peace seems so elusive right now. Peel back the layers of her heart and give her understanding. Settle her and surround her with Your love. Where there is fear or worry, replace it with assurance. Be her peace that passes understanding and guard her heart and mind (Philippians 4:7) as she trusts in You, Lord. Amen.

Lord, fill me with peace in the area of my . . .

_____

_____

_____

_____

Do not be anxious about anything, but in every situation, by prayer and petition, with thanksgiving, present your requests to God.

Philippians 4:6

Lord, I pray for the woman reading this right now who **feels all over the place**. As scattered as she may feel, remind her that You are still in control. You are directing her steps (Proverbs 16:9). You are going before her and leading her even if she doesn't see it right now. Continue to draw her attention to You, Lord. Give her focus and guide her, Lord. Amen.

Lord, I will fix my eyes on You by . . .

_____

_____

_____

_____

_____

In their hearts humans plan their course, but the Lord establishes their steps.

Proverbs 16:9

Lord, I pray for the woman reading this right now who **wishes You would come through for her.** She has been praying so fervently to You, Lord. Pour out Your favor and bless her. In Your kindness and in Your wisdom, answer her prayers and petitions. As she waits on You, align her heart with Yours and give her the desire to want what You will. Be so near to her as she looks to You, Lord. Amen.

Lord, You know what is best, but would You hear my prayer for . . .

_____

_____

_____

_____

If God is for us, who can be against us? He who did not spare his own Son, but gave him up for us all—how will he not also, along with him, graciously give us all things?

Romans 8:31–32

Lord, I pray for the woman reading this right now who **hates who she has become.** Help her to have grace and patience with herself. Remind her You are not in a rush with her. You are full of mercy, and You love her. In Your kindness, lead her to repentance (Romans 2:4). As she turns from what is holding her back from You, continue to change her and grow her closer to You, Lord. Amen.

Lord, to draw closer to You, I know I need to let go of . . .

_____

_____

_____

_____

Or do you show contempt for the riches of his kindness, forbearance and patience, not realizing that God's kindness is intended to lead you to repentance?

Romans 2:4

night
272

Lord, I pray for the woman reading this right now who **is struggling to keep her priorities straight.** Clear her mind and help her to identify what You want for her right now, Lord. Enable her to pursue what is most urgent and most important. Give her wisdom to know what to keep chasing and what to cut out of her life. Help her to stay close to You first and foremost, Lord. Amen.

Lord, I believe the most important things to pursue right now are . . .

_____

_____

_____

_____

_____

Teach us to number our days, that we may gain a heart of wisdom.

Psalm 90:12

Lord, I pray for the woman reading this right now who **can't hear Your voice.** She is listening, but she feels You are nowhere to be found. Silence the noises around her. Eliminate distractions and help her to hear Your voice clearly. Deafen her ears to the voice of the enemy and give her ears to hear the voice of You, Father, her Shepherd who leads her in truth and love, Lord. Amen.

Lord, open my ears to hear You speak to me about . . .

_____

_____

_____

_____

_____

My sheep listen to my voice; I know them, and they follow me. I give them eternal life, and they shall never perish.

John 10:27–28

night
274

Lord, I pray for the woman reading this right now who **received bad news unexpectedly**. Help her to believe that You are still good even when things are bad. Remind her of Your faithfulness in her life. You have come through in the past, and she can trust You to come through now. You won't let her go. You love her and You have a plan for her. Hold her close as she trusts in Your goodness tonight, Lord. Amen.

Lord, I know and believe that You are good because . . .

_____

_____

_____

_____

_____

But you, Lord, are a shield around me, my glory, the One who lifts my head high.

Psalm 3:3

Lord, I pray for the woman reading this right now who **needs rest**. Strengthen her heart and fill her with power through Your Spirit. Dwell in her heart by faith, Lord. Bring rest to her soul by rooting her deeply in Your love—a love that goes beyond knowledge and understanding (Ephesians 3:19). Help her to press pause and find fullness in You, Lord. Amen.

Lord, fill my heart with greater . . .

_____

_____

_____

_____

_____

And to know this love that surpasses knowledge—that you may be filled to the measure of all the fullness of God.

Ephesians 3:19

night
276

Lord, I pray for the woman reading this right now who **doesn't see You working in her life**. Help her to walk in faithfulness and remind her that we don't walk by sight alone. We walk by faith (2 Corinthians 5:7). Transform her heart to trust You more and more, even if she can't see what You are doing. Create in her a new hunger to seek You in Your Word and follow You in obedience to Your will. Open her eyes to see the ways You have been working all along. Give her grace and renew her hunger for You, Lord. Amen.

Lord, even if I can't see You working, I will trust You by . . .

_____

_____

_____

_____

For we live by faith, not by sight.
2 Corinthians 5:7

Lord, I pray for the woman reading this right now who **feels angry**. She wishes she could control her emotions, but it seems so impossible and sometimes pointless to even try. Help her to release her anger to You and allow You to soften her heart. You refine us as we learn from and grow in You, and she can trust You to replace her anger with joy. Take away any desire to get revenge or get even (Romans 12:19) and exchange her anger with mercy tonight, Lord. Amen.

Lord, I release my anger toward . . .

_____

_____

_____

_____

Do not take revenge, my dear friends, but leave room for God's wrath, for it is written: "It is mine to avenge; I will repay," says the Lord.

Romans 12:19

Lord, I pray for the woman reading this right now who **feels hopeless.** Her heart is weary, and she wonders if she will ever feel joy again. Lighten her load and assure her that change is possible, Lord. Allow her to see a new day or a new set of circumstances. Free her from whatever situation she feels she is stuck in and give her the joy of seeing You come through for her. Overwhelm her with Your comfort and Your peace as she trusts in You, Lord. Amen.

Lord, begin a new work in my . . .

_____

_____

_____

_____

The LORD is close to the brokenhearted and saves those who are crushed in spirit. The righteous person may have many troubles, but the LORD delivers him from them all.

Psalm 34:18–19

Lord, I pray for the woman reading this right now who **is struggling to give her past hurt over to You.** Heal her heart and enable her to entrust the past into Your care. Allow Your grace to bring wholeness, Lord. Take her past and heal it so that You can give her a new future shaped by Your love. You have beautiful plans for her life, and she can trust You to use her pain for Your glory. Help her to rest in that tonight, Lord. Amen.

Lord, I know I need to give You the hurt of my . . .

Surely God is my salvation; I will trust and not be afraid. The LORD, the LORD himself, is my strength and my defense; he has become my salvation.

Isaiah 12:2

night
280

Lord, I pray for the woman reading this right now who **is filled with hope for her future**. She has walked a hard road, and she can finally feel the clouds lifting. Don't let her forget Your faithfulness. Let praise and gratitude continue to roll off her lips for all that You have done and will continue to do. Bless her and show her Your kindness as she walks with courage in the days to come, Lord. Amen.

Lord, I will not forget the way You brought me through . . .

_____

_____

_____

_____

_____

Surely your goodness and love will follow me all the days of my life, and I will dwell in the house of the LORD forever.

Psalm 23:6

Lord, I pray for the woman reading this right now who **feels pushed around again and again.** Help her to know where and how to set boundaries so she doesn't feel like she is at the end of her rope. Give her the confidence to stand up to those who are against her with love and grace. She can stand secure in Your love for her and give the best of who she is to those around her. Refresh her strength and faith tonight, Lord. Amen.

Lord, help me to be bold and strong by . . .

_____

_____

_____

_____

But I trust in you, Lord; I say, "You are my God." My times are in your hands; deliver me from the hands of my enemies, from those who pursue me.

Psalm 31:14–15

night
282

Lord, I pray for the woman reading this right now who **wants to start taking better care of herself.** Remind her that it is okay to guard her heart and time and energy. Be a refuge for her and renew her heart by Your Spirit. Don't allow her to become selfish, but do help her to take better care of her own soul so she can love You and others as she should. Overwhelm her with Your peace and rest tonight, Lord. Amen.

Lord, one way I can begin to take better care of myself is by . . .

_____

_____

_____

_____

Look to the Lord and his strength; seek his face always.

Psalm 105:4

Lord, I pray for the woman reading this right now who **wishes the pain would just go away.** She is struggling, and she is tired of feeling this way. Help her to relate her pain to You, Jesus. You not only suffered physically, but You suffered emotionally. So You know her pain and understand her hurt. Meet her, heal her, and comfort her as she comes to You with her sorrow tonight, Lord. Amen.

Lord, I offer the pain of my . . .

_____

_____

_____

_____

_____

Even to your old age and gray hairs I am he, I am he who will sustain you. I have made you and I will carry you; I will sustain you and I will rescue you.

Isaiah 46:4

night
284

Lord, I pray for the woman reading this right now who **is always on edge**. She feels so irritated and isn't sure why. Calm her with Your peace, Lord. Surround her with Your presence. Fight for her and protect her from any attack of the enemy. Open her eyes to the ways she is letting him get a foothold (Ephesians 4:27). Where there is anger or impatience, replace it with Your love. Give her a heart of gratitude and settle her soul tonight, Lord. Amen.

Lord, protect me from feeling . . .

_____

_____

_____

_____

_____

And do not give the devil a foothold.

Ephesians 4:27

Lord, I pray for the woman reading this right now who **has been hurt by others' words**. Soothe her pain, Lord. Drown out the things that have been said about her, those painful words that have pierced her deeply. Replace the lies others have spoken, speaking Your truth over her heart. She is Your precious daughter. Comfort her with Your love for her and help her to sleep soundly tonight, Lord. Amen.

Lord, when I think about what was said, I will . . .

_____

_____

_____

_____

_____

Give ear and come to me; listen, that you may live. I will make an everlasting covenant with you, my faithful love promised to David.

Isaiah 55:3

night
286

Lord, I pray for the woman reading this right now who **is ready to leave her past behind.** Show her what she needs to let go of. Empower her to flee what is entangling her so that she can walk in greater freedom, Lord (Hebrews 12:1). She is a new creation and she can walk confidently in that truth. Give her the wisdom and faith to follow You more closely, trusting that what You have for her is so much better, Lord. Amen.

Lord, as I follow You more closely, I commit to leaving behind . . .

_____

_____

_____

_____

Therefore, since we are surrounded by such a great cloud of witnesses, let us throw off everything that hinders and the sin that so easily entangles. And let us run with perseverance the race marked out for us.

Hebrews 12:1

Lord, I pray for the woman reading this right now who **always feels the pressure to perform.** Help her to seek Your approval alone. Release her and free her from the fear of others, Lord. Motivate her heart to please You and insulate her from the pressure she so often feels. She is chosen by You to bear fruit, and You will give her everything she needs to do so (John 15:16). May she live loved as she follows You, Lord. Amen.

Lord, free me from trying to please . . .

_____

_____

_____

_____

You did not choose me, but I chose you and appointed you so that you might go and bear fruit—fruit that will last—and so that whatever you ask in my name the Father will give you.

John 15:16

Lord, I pray for the woman reading this right now who **feels misunderstood.** No matter how hard she tries, it seems that no one gets her. Don't let her become bitter or resentful, Lord. You know her and understand what her motivation is (Jeremiah 17:10). Encourage and strengthen her heart as she remains true to You. Help her to trust in You and follow You faithfully no matter what anyone else says or does, Lord. Amen.

Lord, guard my heart against becoming . . .

_____

_____

_____

_____

I the L<small>ORD</small> search the heart and examine the mind, to reward each person according to their conduct, according to what their deeds deserve.

Jeremiah 17:10

Lord, I pray for the woman reading this right now who **wishes she could calm her anxious thoughts.** She just wants peace, Lord. Surround her and fight for her in the moments when her mind wanders. Settle and soothe her heart. She doesn't have to worry because You are in complete control of everything in her life. Protect her and reassure her that You are holding her world in Your hands, and You will take care of her, Lord. Amen.

Lord, calm my thoughts of . . .

_____

_____

_____

_____

They will have no fear of bad news; their hearts are steadfast, trusting in the LORD.

Psalm 112:7

night
290

Lord, I pray for the woman reading this right now who **is grateful for all the ways You are working in her life**. Let gratitude overflow in her life. As You have blessed her, let her be a blessing to others, Lord. Pour out Your goodness in and through her, and may her life be a witness to all people (Acts 22:15). Continue to show Your kindness to her as she remains steadfast in her love for You, Lord. Amen.

Lord, I thank You for the way You are working in . . .

_____

_____

_____

_____

_____

You will be his witness to all people of what you have seen and heard.

Acts 22:15

Lord, I pray for the woman reading this right now who **feels this life is unbearable**. She isn't sure how she can get through the days ahead, Lord. Lighten the load she is carrying. Deliver her from feelings of sadness, discouragement, or even despair. Bring freedom and life and hope to what feels so hard and heavy. She needs You desperately. Surround her and hold her close tonight, Lord. Amen.

Lord, deliver me from the weight of . . .

_____

_____

_____

_____

_____

I call as my heart grows faint; lead me to the rock that is higher than I. For you have been my refuge, a strong tower against the foe.

Psalm 61:2–3

night
292

Lord, I pray for the woman reading this right now who **feels she is running in circles**. Give her clarity and help her to see what matters now, Lord. Cut out anything that is not necessary or is a distraction to her. Help her to pursue her greatest priorities first and set aside that which doesn't matter. Calm her heart and surround her with Your peace as she seeks to honor You with her time, Lord. Amen.

Lord, I will stop running in circles by taking the first step to . . .

_____

_____

_____

_____

_____

You will keep in perfect peace those whose minds are steadfast, because they trust in you.

Isaiah 26:3

Lord, I pray for the woman reading this right now who **wishes she could just fix her situation.** Come through for her and solve whatever she feels needs to be changed right now. Help her to turn to You and seek You for relief, Lord. You are the Source of her solution, and You are working all things out for her good (Romans 8:28). Give her eyes to see Your gracious hand in her circumstances, Lord. Amen.

Lord, You alone have the power and wisdom to fix . . .

_____

_____

_____

_____

_____

And we know that in all things God works for the good of those who love him, who have been called according to his purpose.

Romans 8:28

Lord, I pray for the woman reading this right now who **feels she is floundering**. Give her perspective. Don't let her give in to overwhelming thoughts or emotions. What looks and feels like floundering is not always that. You are present and working, even when it seems like You are not. Help her to see the big picture and to remember that no matter what her life looks like, You will not let her walk alone, Lord. Amen.

Lord, help me to keep . . .

_____

_____

_____

_____

Fight the good fight of the faith. Take hold of the eternal life to which you were called when you made your good confession in the presence of many witnesses.

1 Timothy 6:12

Lord, I pray for the woman reading this right now who **gives and gives and gives**. She is at the end of her rope, Lord. Show her how to disengage and set the right kind of boundaries. Remove any guilt she feels when she says no to certain things or people. As she re-engages, help her to do so with healthy and deep and free love. She can love because You first loved her (1 John 4:19). May she look to Your example of serving and sacrifice always, Lord. Amen.

Lord, one way I can begin to establish healthy boundaries is by . . .

_____

_____

_____

_____

_____

We love because he first loved us.

1 John 4:19

night
296

Lord, I pray for the woman reading this right now who **needs good news**. Show Your kindness and favor to her. Hear her prayers, Lord. Be close to her and give her the desires of her heart (Psalm 37:4). Allow her to see the goodness and mercy of Your love by answering her longing for good news. Cover her with Your care and bring assurance to her worried heart tonight, Lord. Amen.

Lord, would You hear my prayers for . . .

_____

_____

_____

_____

_____

Take delight in the LORD, and he will give you the desires of your heart.

Psalm 37:4

Lord, I pray for the woman reading this right now who **is finally finding her hope in You.** Ground her and guard her as she discovers her firm footing in You. Continue to give her the assurance that You are who You say You are. Fill her with faith that what You have promised You will accomplish in her and through her (Psalm 138:8). She can trust You tonight and always, Lord. Amen.

Lord, I am confident that You are the God who will . . .

_____

_____

_____

_____

_____

The LORD will vindicate me; your love, LORD, endures forever—do not abandon the works of your hands.

Psalm 138:8

night
298

Lord, I pray for the woman reading this right now who **is intimidated by the mountain in front of her.** Take her eyes off the mountain. Give her eyes to see You, Lord. Don't let her perspective be clouded by her circumstances. Instead, give her the faith and confidence to see Your character. In her eyes it may look impossible, but nothing is impossible with You, God (Mark 10:27). Help her to find her strength in You, Lord. Amen.

Lord, I will not focus on the mountain, but instead, I will look at . . .

_____

_____

_____

_____

Jesus looked at them and said, "With man this is impossible, but not with God; all things are possible with God."

Mark 10:27

Lord, I pray for the woman reading this right now who **is tired of living a lie**. She is acting like she has it all together, but she doesn't and she is afraid to be vulnerable and admit it. Give her humility and honesty (Psalm 51:6). Help her to rest in Your love for her in all of her poverty. Remind her that You love who she really is, not who she is pretending to be. She can walk securely in the strength You provide, trusting You to take care of what concerns her, Lord. Amen.

Lord, I will no longer pretend to . . .

_____

_____

_____

_____

Yet you desired faithfulness even in the womb; you taught me wisdom in that secret place.

Psalm 51:6

night
300

Lord, I pray for the woman reading this right now who **is questioning Your goodness**. Teach her that Your goodness is not about what she is or isn't going through right now. You are always good and always faithful. You have done great things for her, and she can be filled with joy (Psalm 126:3). Draw her eyes away from her circumstances and let her see Your unchanging character. You see her, and You won't let her go, Lord. Amen.

Lord, I know that You are good because . . .

_____

_____

_____

_____

_____

The LORD has done great things for us, and we are filled with joy.

Psalm 126:3

Lord, I pray for the woman reading this right now who **can't remember the last time she felt joy**. Abide in her. Don't let her be ruled by her emotions, Lord. Anchor her with the truth of Your Word and guide her in Your unchanging love. Be her safe and secure refuge in distress and despair. Overwhelm her with Your deep love for her. She can rest with hope tonight, Lord. Amen.

Lord, I will not be ruled by the emotion of . . .

_____

_____

_____

_____

_____

*May the God of hope fill you with all joy and peace as you trust in him,
so that you may overflow with hope by the power of the Holy Spirit.*

Romans 15:13

Lord, I pray for the woman reading this right now who **is afraid of messing up.** She is struggling to do everything right, and it seems like she is always walking on eggshells. Remind her of Your unconditional love, Lord. She is Your daughter and You have called her Your own (Isaiah 43:1). Show her that she is loved not because of what she does but because of who she is. Help her to accept Your grace tonight, Lord. Amen.

Lord, remind me that Your love does not depend on . . .

_____

_____

_____

_____

But now, this is what the Lord says—he who created you, Jacob, he who formed you, Israel: "Do not fear, for I have redeemed you; I have summoned you by name; you are mine."

Isaiah 43:1

Lord, I pray for the woman reading this right now who **feels she never fits in.** Bless her with people in her life who are true companions and friends she can feel safe with. Give her the wisdom to know how to best cultivate a godly friendship. Show her someone already in her life she can reach out to. Above all, be that Friend to her who is close to her and present with her as she finds acceptance in You, Lord. Amen.

Lord, help me to begin a friendship by taking the step to . . .

_____

_____

_____

_____

_____

Be devoted to one another in love. Honor one another above yourselves.
Romans 12:10

night
304

Lord, I pray for the woman reading this right now who **is amazed at Your goodness in her life**. She has struggled at times, but You have always come through. Continue to fill her with thankfulness and joy. May her love for You overflow to others. May praise always be on her lips (Psalm 34:1) as she points others to Your faithfulness and love, Lord. Help her to hold on to the gratefulness she feels right now, so it will sustain her in the days to come. Amen.

Lord, I praise You for . . .

_____

_____

_____

_____

_____

I will extol the LORD at all times; his praise will always be on my lips.

Psalm 34:1

Lord, I pray for the woman reading this right now who **is longing for a deeper relationship with You.** It feels like she has done all she can to grow closer to You, but You still seem so far away. Teach her that You are with her always (Matthew 28:20). You are working in her life even when she can't see it or feel it. Deepen her faith as she seeks to remain faithful to You. Give her grace and be near to her tonight, Lord. Amen.

Lord, one way I will continue to deepen my faith is . . .

_____

_____

_____

_____

_____

And surely I am with you always, to the very end of the age.
Matthew 28:20

night
306

Lord, I pray for the woman reading this right now who **is hurting**. Comfort and console her tonight. Protect her from trying to soothe her hurt the wrong way, Lord. Bring strength to her and healing to the pain she is experiencing. She can trust that in her day of trouble, You will keep her safe in Your shelter (Psalm 27:5). Be her salvation and so near to her in her time of need, Lord. Amen.

Lord, I will turn to You in my hurt by . . .

_____

_____

_____

_____

_____

For in the day of trouble he will keep me safe in his dwelling; he will hide me in the shelter of his sacred tent and set me high upon a rock.

Psalm 27:5

Lord, I pray for the woman reading this right now who **is tired of going through the motions.** She wants her life to matter, and she worries that it doesn't. Throw off any lie of the enemy that tells her she doesn't have what it takes. She was created for good things that You have planned for her. Squash the discouragement or doubt she is believing. Refresh her faith and rejuvenate her as she seeks to serve You in all things, Lord. Amen.

Lord, I need You to refresh my faith by . . .

_____

_____

_____

_____

For I will pour water on the thirsty land, and streams on the dry ground; I will pour out my Spirit on your offspring, and my blessing on your descendants.

Isaiah 44:3

night
308

Lord, I pray for the woman reading this right now who **needs patience**. This isn't something she can produce. Patience comes from You, Lord. Come, Holy Spirit, and fill her. Grow the fruit of patience in her heart with whatever circumstances she is facing right now. Help her to be faithful to You even when it feels like she is waiting forever. She can trust You. Give her peace tonight, Lord. Amen.

Lord, give me patience in the area of . . .

_____

_____

_____

_____

_____

The LORD is good to those whose hope is in him, to the one who seeks him; it is good to wait quietly for the salvation of the LORD.

Lamentations 3:25–26

Lord, I pray for the woman reading this right now who **has stopped serving You.** She has stepped away from the church and You because of past hurt. Out of love for her, call her back to You in repentance and faith. Bring healing to the hurting places in her heart. Confront any idols she has built in her life. Tear down those things in her life that are leading her away from You and show her that following You is the good life, Lord. Amen.

Lord, I confess that I haven't been serving You because . . .

_____

_____

_____

_____

Repent, then, and turn to God, so that your sins may be wiped out, that times of refreshing may come from the Lord.

Acts 3:19

night
310

Lord, I pray for the woman reading this right now who **hates her life**. She wishes things were different, and she feels like there is no way to change who she has become and where she is. Fix her eyes on You and all that You have done, are doing, and have promised to do, Lord. Root out bitterness and pull any weeds of discontent. Be her greatest treasure and the source of her deepest joy. Increase faith in her life as she trusts You with where You have her, Lord. Amen.

Lord, instead of focusing on what I don't have, I will give thanks for . . .

_____

_____

_____

_____

That is why, for Christ's sake, I delight in weaknesses, in insults, in hardships, in persecutions, in difficulties. For when I am weak, then I am strong.

2 Corinthians 12:10

night
311

Lord, I pray for the woman reading this right now who **wishes she understood Your Word better**. She studies and reads, but she feels so inadequate. Pour out Your Spirit and give her spiritual understanding. Teach her to not only hear Your Word but obey it (James 1:22). Continue to give her a hunger for Your truth and make her heart like fertile soil for Your truth to grow. Be with her as she seeks to learn from You, Lord. Amen.

Lord, I will commit to honoring Your Word by . . .

_____

_____

_____

_____

_____

Do not merely listen to the word, and so deceive yourselves. Do what it says.
James 1:22

night
312

Lord, I pray for the woman reading this right now who **needs Your grace**. In her weakness, strengthen her. It is You, Lord, who is working in her life, and she can trust You to renew her heart. Help her to look to You and to rely on Your grace in greater ways. As she relies on You, give her the power she needs to accomplish what You have for her, Lord. Amen.

Lord, I need Your grace most in . . .

_____

_____

_____

_____

_____

And God is able to bless you abundantly, so that in all things at all times, having all that you need, you will abound in every good work.

2 Corinthians 9:8

Lord, I pray for the woman reading this right now who **is struggling with resentment**. Guard her heart against envy, Lord. Show her the ways she is focusing on what others have instead of what You have given her and fill her with gratitude instead. Give her eyes to see all that You have provided for her and help her to rejoice over these good things in her life. Soften her heart as she surrenders to You tonight, Lord. Amen.

Lord, I give You thanks for . . .

_____

_____

_____

_____

_____

Praise the LORD, my soul, and forget not all his benefits.

Psalm 103:2

night
314

Lord, I pray for the woman reading this right now who **is disappointed in herself**. Bring her relief from discouragement. Don't let her be overcome by her failure. Instead, take her eyes off of herself and off of her sin and refocus her attention on You, Jesus. It is who You are that fills us with joy and hope. Make that clear to her tonight. You love her, and You will forgive her if she comes to You (1 John 1:9). Envelop her with grace as she hands her disappointments to You, Lord. Amen.

Lord, instead of focusing on my failure, I will focus on . . .

_____

_____

_____

_____

If we confess our sins, he is faithful and just and will forgive us our sins and purify us from all unrighteousness.

1 John 1:9

Lord, I pray for the woman reading this right now who **wants to live faithfully right where You have her.** Open her eyes and soften her heart to those around her. Empower her to love greatly, even in the small things. You have equipped her with every good thing to do Your will (Hebrews 13:21). Give her a growing awareness of Your presence and help her to do all things for Your glory, Lord. Amen.

Lord, one way of remembering Your presence right where I am is to . . .

_____

_____

_____

_____

Equip you with everything good for doing his will, and may he work in us what is pleasing to him, through Jesus Christ, to whom be glory for ever and ever. Amen.

Hebrews 13:21

night
316

Lord, I pray for the woman reading this right now who **is in need of a respite**. She has been through so much, and she needs a break. Bring rest where she feels weary. No matter the path, give her the right feet to walk humbly and faithfully. She can come with confidence to the throne of grace and find mercy in her time of need (Hebrews 4:16). Shelter her as she finds help in You, Lord. Amen.

Lord, give me relief from . . .

Let us then approach God's throne of grace with confidence, so that we may receive mercy and find grace to help us in our time of need.

Hebrews 4:16

Lord, I pray for the woman reading this right now who **feels emotionally unstable**. She finds herself laughing one minute and crying the next, and she just can't seem to get it together. Draw her to You and help her to see it is okay for her to be honest with You. As she brings her emotions to You, give her the wisdom of knowing how she should feel. Give her courage to seek help if she needs it and help her to learn to honor You in this area, Lord. Amen.

Lord, teach me how to deal with the emotion of . . .

_____

_____

_____

_____

The LORD is near to all who call on him, to all who call on him in truth. He fulfills the desires of those who fear him; he hears their cry and saves them.

Psalm 145:18–19

night
318

Lord, I pray for the woman reading this right now who **wishes she could withdraw from everyone and everything.** This season has been so hard, and she knows she needs others, but many times she just wants to hide. Protect her from isolating herself from those who are there for her. Lead her to the people who can encourage and support her. Give her courage to be vulnerable with others and show her Your love through them as she is present, Lord. Amen.

Lord, I will resist the temptation to withdraw by . . .

_____

_____

_____

_____

Two are better than one, because they have a good return for their labor:
If either of them falls down, one can help the other up.

Ecclesiastes 4:9–10

Lord, I pray for the woman reading this right now who **feels angry about how she's been treated by someone she trusted.** Be her defender and help her to entrust herself to You, the One who judges justly (1 Peter 2:23). Let her live faithfully for You and allow her life to be the best argument for the truth. Give her the courage to forgive as You have forgiven her tonight, Lord. Amen.

Lord, instead of wanting to get even, I will . . .

_____

_____

_____

_____

_____

When they hurled their insults at him, he did not retaliate; when he suffered, he made no threats. Instead, he entrusted himself to him who judges justly.

1 Peter 2:23

night
320

Lord, I pray for the woman reading this right now who **wishes You would speak to her**. Help her to recognize Your voice. Help her to find solitude when she can just sit and listen. Speak to her in her circumstances and speak to her through Your Word, Lord. Surround her with the right people who will share Your truth with her. Give her the answers she is longing for in this season, Lord. Amen.

Lord, speak to me about . . .

_____

_____

_____

_____

_____

Here I am! I stand at the door and knock. If anyone hears my voice and opens the door, I will come in and eat with that person, and they with me.

Revelation 3:20

Lord, I pray for the woman reading this right now who **feels unlovable**. Silence the voice of the enemy and amplify the voice of Your Spirit. She is Your daughter, and she is loved. She can rest in that. You love her and have promised never to leave her (Hebrews 13:5). May You encourage her with this truth and be a **fortress for her** when she doubts it. Come close to her tonight as she finds assurance in Your embrace, Lord. Amen.

Lord, when I feel unlovable, I will remind myself that . . .

_____

_____

_____

_____

_____

God has said, "Never will I leave you; never will I forsake you."
Hebrews 13:5

Lord, I pray for the woman reading this right now who **is finally ready to come clean.** She has pretended for too long and she is ready to give her life to You. As she pursues a life set apart for You, strengthen her and protect her. Teach her to focus on today and the small things in her life she can surrender to You. Go before her and surround her on every side. Give her a passion for Your Word and a genuine surrender to Your way, Lord. Amen.

Lord, I am ready to give You my whole life by . . .

_____

_____

_____

_____

When Jesus spoke again to the people, he said, "I am the light of the world. Whoever follows me will never walk in darkness, but will have the light of life."

John 8:12

night
323

Lord, I pray for the woman reading this right now who **is floundering because of all she has on her plate**. It feels like too much and she doesn't even know where to begin. Calm her heart tonight, Lord. Help her to stop whatever she is in the middle of, take a deep breath, and turn her tasks over to You. Give her Your power to accomplish what You have for her (Ephesians 3:20). Help her to trust You with what she can't do or doesn't have time for. And help her to enjoy the process along the way. Be her strength and peace because she can't do it alone, Lord. Amen.

Lord, give me peace with all that I have on my plate and help me . . .

_____

_____

_____

Now to him who is able to do immeasurably more than all we ask or imagine, according to his power that is at work within us.

Ephesians 3:20

night
324

Lord, I pray for the woman reading this right now who **just needs some space to breathe.** Her life has been moving at a frantic pace, and she can't keep up. Take the pressure to perform or deliver in a certain way away from her. Give her wisdom on how she can create more space for her soul to flourish. Allow her to rest in You and Your plans and help her to find peace tonight as she sleeps, Lord. Amen.

Lord, I will seek ways to create space for my soul by . . .

_____

_____

_____

_____

_____

The Lord replied, "My Presence will go with you, and I will give you rest."

Exodus 33:14

Lord, I pray for the woman reading this right now who **is upset by the behavior of other Christians in her life.** She is trying to live a set-apart life, and these people can make it really hard to "be holy." Calm her frustrations, Lord. Help her to surrender the expectations of others to You and trust that You are in control. Give her the freedom to create distance and boundaries where they need to be. Bless her with friends who will spur her on in her relationship with You, Lord. Amen.

Lord, I will surrender these relationships to You and . . .

_____

_____

_____

_____

Do not conform to the pattern of this world, but be transformed by the renewing of your mind.

Romans 12:2

Lord, I pray for the woman reading this right now who **feels angry with You**. Teach her that it is okay to bring her anger to You, but not okay to remain angry *at* You. Meet her in the midst of her pain and disappointment, Lord. Soften her heart and open her eyes to what You want to do in her heart. Overwhelm her with Your love for her even now. She can come with surrender to You, Lord. Amen.

Lord, I believe that the real source of my anger may be . . .

_____

_____

_____

_____

_____

Why, my soul, are you downcast? Why so disturbed within me? Put your hope in God, for I will yet praise him, my Savior and my God.

Psalm 42:11

Lord, I pray for the woman reading this right now who **is indecisive.**
No matter how many times she prays and ponders, she can't seem to
make up her mind. Give her courage and boldness to act. Remind her
that You are faithful. Regardless of her plans, Your purposes always
prevail (Proverbs 19:21). You work through all her choices. You will
direct her steps and lead her to where You want her, Lord. Amen.

Lord, in faith, I know I need to decide to . . .

_____

_____

_____

_____

_____

*Many are the plans in a person's heart, but it is the LORD's purpose that
prevails.*

Proverbs 19:21

Lord, I pray for the woman reading this right now who **wants to let go of her unhealthy coping mechanisms.** Bring freedom and release her from the bondage she is under. Soften her heart to follow You fully with her life. Empower her through Your Spirit to entrust whatever hurt she has experienced to You. You are faithful to bring healing to her heart. Cover her with Your grace and be so close to her as she gives her struggles to You, Lord. Amen.

Lord, help me to release . . .

_____

_____

_____

_____

The LORD has anointed me to proclaim good news to the poor. He has sent me to bind up the brokenhearted, to proclaim freedom for the captives and release from darkness for the prisoners.

Isaiah 61:1

Lord, I pray for the woman reading this right now who **feels uncertain**. She is seeking Your way, Lord, but it doesn't seem clear. Give her confidence that You really are in control of every detail. She doesn't have to worry or fear that she is just wandering through life. You have a plan for her, and You can be trusted with that plan. Give her vision to see You and Your will, Lord. Amen.

Lord, give me clarity to know what You want me to do with . . .

_____

_____

_____

_____

_____

Show me your ways, Lord, teach me your paths. Guide me in your truth and teach me, for you are God my Savior, and my hope is in you all day long.
Psalm 25:4–5

Lord, I pray for the woman reading this right now who **is crushed by her circumstances**. Restore her and be close to her. Comfort and soothe her pain, Lord. Remind her that her current reality is not her final reality. You have more for her, and even when it feels hopeless, there is hope to be found in You. You will bring her through whatever she is facing. Overwhelm her with deep peace and assurance tonight, Lord. Amen.

Lord, I am believing You to bring good out of . . .

_____

_____

_____

_____

Yet this I call to mind and therefore I have hope: Because of the LORD's great love we are not consumed, for his compassions never fail. They are new every morning; great is your faithfulness.

Lamentations 3:21–23

Lord, I pray for the woman reading this right now who **is determined to make things right**. She deeply desires to bring restoration to an area of her life. Give her courage and humility as she seeks wholeness. Lead her with wisdom to know how to right and restore those areas of her life that need to be made new. Bring freedom and hope to her heart as she takes these steps tonight, Lord. Amen.

Lord, I will be intentional to take the first step in restoring . . .

_____

_____

_____

_____

_____

But whoever lives by the truth comes into the light, so that it may be seen plainly that what they have done has been done in the sight of God.

John 3:21

night
332

Lord, I pray for the woman reading this right now who **has unresolved trauma that haunts her**. Surround her with Your presence and deliver her from despair. Protect her from discouragement or apathy. Give her the courage to seek help to heal these hidden parts of her life. You can make all things new even when it feels impossible. Fill her with hope, Lord. Help her to begin again and trust You will take care of her every step of the way, Lord. Amen.

Lord, I will seek help and release to You . . .

_____

_____

_____

_____

For everyone born of God overcomes the world. This is the victory that has overcome the world, even our faith.

1 John 5:4

Lord, I pray for the woman reading this right now who **has a heart that has grown cold to You**. Give her insight into why her heart is far from You right now. If it is sin, out of Your kindness, draw her out of it, Lord. Restore the joy of her salvation and give her a new hunger and longing for You. Open her eyes to the wonder of Your grace and love as she takes an honest look at where she is in her relationship with You, Lord. Amen.

Lord, as I examine my heart, I believe it has grown cold because . . .

_____

_____

_____

_____

_____

Never be lacking in zeal, but keep your spiritual fervor, serving the Lord.

Romans 12:11

night
334

Lord, I pray for the woman reading this right now who **wishes she could change her past**. Release her from the feelings of guilt that plague her. Lift the weight of past mistakes. Refresh her and remind her that she is loved by You. Help her to focus on the present, Lord. Give her eyes to see Your mercy in this moment and what You are doing in her today—and what You will do through her tomorrow. Encourage her heart tonight, Lord. Amen.

Lord, I give You the guilt of . . .

_____

_____

_____

_____

For as high as the heavens are above the earth, so great is his love for those who fear him; as far as the east is from the west, so far has he removed our transgressions from us.

Psalm 103:11–12

Lord, I pray for the woman reading this right now who **is afraid to reach out in her time of need.** Would you enable her to see the gift of being a part of Your body, the church? She can have confidence that You will take care of her, and Your people will be a witness to Your goodness through service to one another. Give her the courage and humility to take the first step and find someone to help her. Allow her to receive joyfully what You have for her, Lord. Amen.

Lord, I will ask for help by . . .

_____

_____

_____

_____

For just as each of us has one body with many members, and these members do not all have the same function, so in Christ we, though many, form one body, and each member belongs to all the others.

Romans 12:4–5

night
336

Lord, I pray for the woman reading this right now who **is struggling to depend on You.** Bring humility and grow greater confidence in You within her. Help her to see that You possess the wisdom, power, and resources she does not have. As she depends on You in greater ways, show Your faithfulness to her. Give her grace as she lays down her strength for Yours, Lord. Amen.

Lord, I know I need to depend on You more with my . . .

_____

_____

_____

_____

_____

But I trust in your unfailing love; my heart rejoices in your salvation. I will sing the Lord's praise, for he has been good to me.

Psalm 13:5–6

Lord, I pray for the woman reading this right now who **feels disappointed with where she is in life.** Help her to see that life is not a race. Encourage her with the truth that You are patient with her, and Your work will not go unfinished (Philippians 1:6). Don't allow her to give in to doubt or discouragement. Give her the strength to keep walking with You and trusting You for what You have in store for her tonight, Lord. Amen.

Lord, I will not be overcome by the discouragement of . . .

_____

_____

_____

_____

Being confident of this, that he who began a good work in you will carry it on to completion until the day of Christ Jesus.

Philippians 1:6

night
338

Lord, I pray for the woman reading this right now who **needs the faith to surrender her situation to You**. Convince her that You are not only powerful but that You are also good and wise. You are trustworthy, Lord. Remind her of Your character and Your promise to never leave her nor forsake her. You are here for her in her time of need (Psalm 9:9) and You won't let her go. Help her to believe that tonight, Lord. Amen.

Lord, open my hands and allow me to release . . .

_____

_____

_____

_____

_____

The Lord is a refuge for the oppressed, a stronghold in times of trouble.

Psalm 9:9

Lord, I pray for the woman reading this right now who **has an unsettled heart**. Let her mind be controlled by Your Spirit and not by her flesh. Keep her from living apart from Your love. You alone are peace. Guard her heart and mind and help her to trust that You are working during this time when things just don't feel right. Increase her faith and hope in who You are and what You can do no matter how she feels, Lord. Amen.

Lord, I will allow You to control my thoughts by learning to . . .

_____

_____

_____

_____

But the fruit of the Spirit is love, joy, peace, forbearance, kindness, goodness, faithfulness, gentleness and self-control.

Galatians 5:22–23

night
340

Lord, I pray for the woman reading this right now who **doesn't know how to move on from all she has been through.** Focus her attention on today alone. Don't allow her to be overwhelmed about the future. Give her the wisdom to take one day and one step at a time. The rest is in Your hands, Lord. She can trust You for today and tomorrow. Be her strength and guide as she discovers healing in You, Lord. Amen.

Lord, one simple step I can take to move on is . . .

_____

_____

_____

_____

I have been crucified with Christ and I no longer live, but Christ lives in me. The life I now live in the body, I live by faith in the Son of God, who loved me and gave himself for me.

Galatians 2:20

night
341

Lord, I pray for the woman reading this right now who **wonders if this is it**. She has spent her life following You, and her faith feels so boring and dead. Awaken her faith, Lord. Give her a new and greater joy that comes from serving You. Resurrect her passion for You and remind her of what You have called her to. She can find fresh life in following close to You no matter what her emotions tell her. Help her to feel Your presence near tonight, Lord. Amen.

Lord, I am asking You to resurrect in me a . . .

_____

_____

_____

_____

_____

Be joyful in hope, patient in affliction, faithful in prayer.
Romans 12:12

night
342

Lord, I pray for the woman reading this right now who **wants to believe You will take care of her.** She has been through so much, but she knows You are good and she is trying to trust You. Hold her in Your hands. Protect her and provide for her in every way. Make her aware of Your presence and love her through what she is going through now. When she feels unsteady, be her Rock (Psalm 18:2) and help her to find security in You, Lord. Amen.

Lord, I know You will take care of me because . . .

_____

_____

_____

_____

The LORD is my rock, my fortress and my deliverer; my God is my rock, in whom I take refuge, my shield and the horn of my salvation, my stronghold.

Psalm 18:2

Lord, I pray for the woman reading this right now who **is wrestling with what to do with her life**. Don't let her be confused or consumed by the future. Teach her to focus on obeying Your will today. Whatever comes her way, enable her to do it with love for You and love for others. As she follows You, continue to give her clarity on what is next, Lord. Amen.

Lord, in love, help me to be faithful today by . . .

_____

_____

_____

_____

_____

And this is love: that we walk in obedience to his commands. As you have heard from the beginning, his command is that you walk in love.

2 John 1:6

Lord, I pray for the woman reading this right now who **has a heavy heart.** Jesus, You are the man of sorrows (Isaiah 53:3). Remind her that You know exactly what it's like to suffer. Help her to know You more deeply and more intimately in her sorrow. Lift the heavy burden she is carrying, Lord. Be her rest and comfort. Anchor her in Your loving care tonight, Lord. Amen.

Lord, I give to You the heavy burden of . . .

_____

_____

_____

_____

He was despised and rejected by mankind, a man of suffering, and familiar with pain. Like one from whom people hide their faces he was despised, and we held him in low esteem.

Isaiah 53:3

Lord, I pray for the woman reading this right now who **feels "out of it."** She wants to be present, but her heart and mind are so distant. Things seem foggy all the time, and she is struggling. Help her to turn her attention to You and where You are working in her life now. Give her an energy and a longing to be engaged with her current circumstances. Open her eyes to the areas of her life where she needs rest to feel fully present and refreshed. Be her strength tonight and always, Lord. Amen.

Lord, help me to intentionally seek rest in order to be present in . . .

_____

_____

_____

And if the Spirit of him who raised Jesus from the dead is living in you, he who raised Christ from the dead will also give life to your mortal bodies because of his Spirit who lives in you.

Romans 8:11

night
346

Lord, I pray for the woman reading this right now who **is making bad choices**. Soften her heart and open her eyes. Help her to see the path, the road away from life, that she is on. It is Your kindness that leads her to repentance (Romans 2:4). Lead her to You, Jesus, the One who has promised us real and abundant life. Convict her, but also comfort her tonight, Lord. Amen.

Lord, I confess the sin of . . .

_____

_____

_____

_____

Or do you show contempt for the riches of his kindness, forbearance and patience, not realizing that God's kindness is intended to lead you to repentance?

Romans 2:4

Lord, I pray for the woman reading this right now who **is wrestling with her faith**. Fill her with Your Spirit. Increase her faith. Give her more hope. Enlarge her love for You. Don't let her believe the lie that turning away from You is the answer. Instead, draw her closer and deeper to You, Lord. Turn any doubts she has into greater devotion as she comes honestly to You tonight, Lord. Amen.

Lord, even though I am struggling with my faith, I will continue to . . .

_____

_____

_____

_____

_____

Let us hold unswervingly to the hope we profess, for he who promised is faithful.

Hebrews 10:23

Lord, I pray for the woman reading this right now who **feels shame because of what has been done to her.** She is loved and cherished by You. Clothe her in the secure and safe covering of Your grace. Remind her, Jesus, that You have made her clean by Your death and resurrection. She is loved and accepted by You (Ephesians 1:6), and You see her for who she really is. Be so near to her and help her to find security in Your constant care, Lord. Amen.

Lord, I will rest in knowing that You have covered my shame of . . .

_____

_____

_____

_____

To the praise of his glorious grace, which he has freely given us in the One he loves.

Ephesians 1:6

Lord, I pray for the woman reading this right now who **feels her life is unmanageable.** Sustain her with Your love and wisdom. When she doesn't feel she can keep it all together, remind her that You are in control. Carry her and provide what she can't on her own. Rid her mind of doubt and discouragement and fill it with greater dependence on You. Help her to find solace as she depends on You tonight, Lord. Amen.

Lord, I need You to help me carry . . .

_____

_____

_____

_____

For I am the LORD your God who takes hold of your right hand and says to you, Do not fear; I will help you.

Isaiah 41:13

Lord, I pray for the woman reading this right now who **doesn't know where to turn**. She feels lost and isn't sure how to find her footing. Give her faith to turn to You. And give her wisdom to turn to someone she trusts. Protect her and remind her that she needs to surround herself with others who can love her, pray for her, and be there for her (1 Peter 4:8–10). Help her as she seeks out support from others and ultimately support from You, Lord. Amen.

Lord, I will take the step of turning to someone else by . . .

_____

_____

_____

Above all, love each other deeply, because love covers over a multitude of sins. Offer hospitality to one another without grumbling. Each of you should use whatever gift you have received to serve others, as faithful stewards of God's grace in its various forms.

1 Peter 4:8–10

Lord, I pray for the woman reading this right now who **wants to experience Your presence.** Be near her and make her aware of Your closeness in a tangible way. When she can't feel Your presence, increase her faith. Remind her that Your Spirit dwells in her (1 Corinthians 3:16). Grow her trust and give her the courage to keep following You no matter what, Lord. Amen.

Lord, help me to be aware of Your presence when I . . .

_____

_____

_____

_____

_____

Don't you know that you yourselves are God's temple and that God's Spirit dwells in your midst?

1 Corinthians 3:16

night
352

Lord, I pray for the woman reading this right now who **feels she is losing control**. Teach her she doesn't have to hold on to everything perfectly. Even when she feels like she doesn't have control, You do. Bring balance to the places in her heart that feel unsteady. Help her to have a heart of surrender that trusts in Your perfect plan for her, Lord. Amen.

Lord, I give You control of . . .

My flesh and my heart may fail, but God is the strength of my heart and my portion forever.

Psalm 73:26

Lord, I pray for the woman reading this right now who **feels confused by a situation in her life.** You promise that You will give wisdom when she asks (James 1:5), so give her direction. Open her eyes and direct her thoughts to know what she is supposed to do. Give her the clarity and courage to move forward in the situation she is in with confidence that You are leading her, Lord. Amen.

Lord, give me wisdom so I know what to do in . . .

_____

_____

_____

_____

_____

If any of you lacks wisdom, you should ask God, who gives generously to all without finding fault, and it will be given to you.

James 1:5

night
354

Lord, I pray for the woman reading this right now who **has been treated poorly by those in authority**. Hear her prayers and her hurts tonight. Be close to her as a faithful and true friend. Comfort her as a reliable and kind companion. Don't let her believe the words that have wounded her or be devastated by the actions taken against her. Let her know and experience what You say about her. She is Your beautiful daughter, and You love her. She can rest in that truth, Lord. Amen.

Lord, speak to me and remind me that I am . . .

_____

_____

_____

Praise be to the God and Father of our Lord Jesus Christ, the Father of compassion and the God of all comfort, who comforts us in all our troubles, so that we can comfort those in any trouble with the comfort we ourselves receive from God.

2 Corinthians 1:3–4

Lord, I pray for the woman reading this right now who **has sacrificed so much to follow You.** Keep her eyes on You, Jesus. Remind her of how You have loved her at her best and at her worst. Continue to increase her love for You and her desire to give her life as an offering of love. Help her to stay focused on loving and not just being loved. Surround her with Your peace and give her favor as she serves You, Lord. Amen.

Lord, I will stay focused on loving You by . . .

_____

_____

_____

_____

But even if I am being poured out like a drink offering on the sacrifice and service coming from your faith, I am glad and rejoice with all of you.

Philippians 2:17

night
356

Lord, I pray for the woman reading this right now who **has grown jaded**. Peel away the layers of her heart that have become hardened. You are forgiving and good, abounding in love to all who call on You (Psalm 86:5). Chip away at any resentment or bitterness she is experiencing. Where there is unforgiveness, bring love and mercy. Help her to find joy again in following You and loving others, Lord. Amen.

Lord, soften my heart in the area of . . .

_____

_____

_____

_____

_____

You, Lord, are forgiving and good, abounding in love to all who call to you.

Psalm 86:5

Lord, I pray for the woman reading this right now who **has become complacent in her faith**. Bring conviction where it is necessary. Revive her and help her to see the distractions in her life that may have deadened her faith or turned her eyes from You. Awaken her desire to follow You with everything she is and give her a hunger for what really matters most, Lord. Amen.

Lord, forgive me for becoming complacent in . . .

_____

_____

_____

_____

_____

For this reason I remind you to fan into flame the gift of God, which is in you through the laying on of my hands.

2 Timothy 1:6

night
358

Lord, I pray for the woman reading this right now who **feels she is drowning**. Raise her and set her feet on more solid footing. Bring relief to the areas of her life where she feels overwhelmed. Allow her to see why it feels like she is drowning and identify the areas where she may need to make a change. Help her to keep her eyes on You no matter what her circumstances are. Support her as she holds on to You, Lord. Amen.

Lord, one change I know I need to make is . . .

_____

_____

_____

_____

When you pass through the waters, I will be with you; and when you pass through the rivers, they will not sweep over you. When you walk through the fire, you will not be burned; the flames will not set you ablaze.

Isaiah 43:2

night
359

Lord, I pray for the woman reading this right now who **is wrestling with a bad decision**. Give her grace to be gentle with herself but humble enough to release to You what she has done. Saturate her with Your mercy and tenderness. Teach her to rest in Your grace and yet feel compelled to grow closer to You in faithfulness. Be so near to her tonight as she surrenders fully to You, Lord. Amen.

Lord, I will be gentle with myself by . . .

_____

_____

_____

_____

Therefore, there is now no condemnation for those who are in Christ Jesus, because through Christ Jesus the law of the Spirit who gives life has set you free from the law of sin and death.

Romans 8:1–2

night
360

Lord, I pray for the woman reading this right now who **wants to stop numbing her pain.** She has felt so uneasy for so long and she has turned to everything but You. Help her to experience the peace and calm that You offer, Lord. Guard her heart and her mind from any attack of the enemy. Surround her with Your Spirit and allow her mind to be controlled not by her own flesh but by You. Give her the strength to throw off anything other than You tonight, Lord. Amen.

Lord, I want to give over all the things I've turned to besides You by . . .

_____

_____

_____

_____

The mind governed by the flesh is death, but the mind governed by the Spirit is life and peace.

Romans 8:6

Lord, I pray for the woman reading this right now who **feels she needs to be perfect**. Remind her that You alone are perfect (2 Corinthians 5:21). Guard her heart from having to be right or to do everything right. Your faithfulness prevails in her life. Help her to find peace by doing what she can and leaving the rest to You. You are the One who is in control and working through her. She can find peace in that truth tonight, Lord. Amen.

Lord, I don't need to be perfect in my . . .

_____

_____

_____

_____

God made him who had no sin to be sin for us, so that in him we might become the righteousness of God.

2 Corinthians 5:21

night
362

Lord, I pray for the woman reading this right now who **is ready for a new start.** Show her what that new start is. Give her not only enthusiasm but also endurance to follow You into a different season. Prepare her for what is to come. Help her to find her strength in You as she walks in faithfulness to You, Lord. Amen.

Lord, go before me and prepare me for a new start with . . .

_____

_____

_____

_____

_____

See, I am doing a new thing! Now it springs up; do you not perceive it? I am making a way in the wilderness and streams in the wasteland.

Isaiah 43:19

Lord, I pray for the woman reading this right now who **needs to forgive herself.** Comfort her with Your mercy. Reassure her that she can be honest with You about who she really is. Your love is patient and kind (1 Corinthians 13:4). Allow her to rest in Your unconditional acceptance of her no matter what she has done. You bring healing and hope to every area of her life. Purify her heart as she submits to You tonight, Lord. Amen.

Lord, I know I need to forgive myself for . . .

_____

_____

_____

_____

Love is patient, love is kind. It does not envy, it does not boast, it is not proud.

1 Corinthians 13:4

night
364

Lord, I pray for the woman reading this right now who **is afraid to speak up for You.** Fill her to fullness with faith from You. Guard her against becoming too focused on what others think. Don't let her be moved by people's opinions of her. Give her courage to stand for truth but let her do so in love and humility (Colossians 4:6) as she walks faithfully with You, Lord. Amen.

Lord, give me the courage to speak for You in the area of . . .

_____

_____

_____

_____

_____

Let your conversation be always full of grace, seasoned with salt, so that you may know how to answer everyone.

Colossians 4:6

night
365

Lord, I pray for the woman reading this right now who **is excited about what You have in store for her**. Show her Your favor. Bless her and provide for her, Lord. You are making a way for her and calling her into a new season. Pour out Your Spirit (Acts 2:17) and empower her to walk faithfully into this next chapter of her life. Give her grace as she gives her life to You, Lord. Amen.

Lord, help me to follow You into . . .

_____

_____

_____

_____

In the last days, God says, I will pour out my Spirit on all people. Your sons and daughters will prophesy, your young men will see visions, your old men will dream dreams.

Acts 2:17

Ruth Schwenk is the founder of the popular blog *TheBetterMom .com* and co-founder with her husband, Patrick, of the podcast *Rootlike Faith*. She is the author of several books, including *Trusting God in All the Things*, co-authored with Karen Ehman; *In a Boat in the Middle of a Lake*, co-authored with Patrick; and her bestselling devo, *The Better Mom Devotional*. Ruth lives with her husband and their four kids in the dreamy college town of Ann Arbor, Michigan.